FOOD
FOR
FRIENDS

FOOD FOR FRIENDS

More Than 75 Easy Recipes from a Brooklyn Kitchen

LINNÉA JOHANSSON

Translated by Gun Penhoat

Skyhorse Publishing

Translation copyright © 2016 by Skyhorse Publishing

Originally published as *Recept Från Sena Kvällar I New York* by Norstedts, Sweden.
Copyright © 2014 by Linnéa Johansson. Published by agreement with Norstedts Agency.

Skyhorse Publishing books may be purchased in bulk at special discounts for sales promotion, corporate gifts, fund-raising, or educational purposes. Special editions can also be created to specifications. For details, contact the Special Sales Department, Skyhorse Publishing, 307 West 36th Street, 11th Floor, New York, NY 10018 or info@skyhorsepublishing.com.

Skyhorse® and Skyhorse Publishing® are registered trademarks of Skyhorse Publishing, Inc.®, a Delaware corporation.

Visit our website at www.skyhorsepublishing.com.

10 9 8 7 6 5 4 3 2 1
Library of Congress Cataloging-in-Publication Data is available on file.

Photography, food: Adrian Mueller
Photography, people: Dan McMahon
Art Director: Tadeu Magalhäes
Illustrations: Tove Eklund
Repro: Elanders Fälth & Hässler

US Edition cover design: Laura Klynstra

Print ISBN: 978-1-63450-637-3
Ebook ISBN: 978-1-63450-638-0

Printed in China

Contents

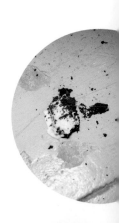

Classics

There's a reason why classics became classics—they work. *BASTA.*

I loved my time with my grandmother in her kitchen on the tiny island of Tjörn in Sweden. That woman was out of this world, and for her a three-course-meal was not just something you put together for Sunday dinner; it was on the table every night. She served every meal with gusto. Most of the food in her kitchen, from horseradish to grapes, came from her own garden. You could even call her an 80s precursor to the locovore movement. But dinner wasn't the only meal that came with a dash of overkill from Grandma. Breakfast was sandwiches made from freshly baked bread accompanied by tea. Then, slightly unexpectedly, came breakfast number two, consisting of yogurt and homemade muesli. After what felt like fifteen minutes, a hot lunch was ready. On top of this, she happily threw in a coffee break or two with homemade cinnamon buns or cookies—just so you wouldn't go hungry for a single second! She was an absolute machine who hated the thought of store-bought foods; she baked her own bread; she canned her own jams; and she roasted her own muesli.

So where the hell did Grandma learn to do all of this?

Well, Grandma's mom, my great-grandmother Ebon, was no slouch in the kitchen either. She started working at a young age at the butcher shop in the Bazar Alliance in Gothenburg, Sweden. (Yes, I like to brag that I'm a third-generation butcher). After twenty years of working her ass off, Grandma bought the shop, renamed it Ebon's, and it became one of the main attractions of Gothenburg's market hall. As irony would have it, I'm not the first person in my family to put out a cookbook. Great-Granny Ebon published one as well.

You might think that this would be enough of a food heritage, but no! I inherited even more good food genes from my father, one of the most creative cooks I've ever met. Jokingly known around town as "Gothenburg Jesus," on account of his luxurious

beard. Without second thought to the six-hour time difference, he can call me in the middle of the night in New York and passionately tell me every detail of his latest food pairings, such as lingonberry and avocado compote. Though his combos always sound a bit strange, he swears by them.

I spent a lot of time cooking with my dad in his messy kitchen. One of my favorite dishes was his homemade crepes. The higher he flipped them into the air, the more impressed I was, so naturally some crepes always ended up on the ceiling light. Thus the "lamp crepe" was born. Here, the feat was that you had to remove the crepes from the fixture while they were still in good enough shape to be cooked on the flip side. Upon our failure, our dog Lord lucked out, as he got to eat the remains. And thus the "doggie crepe" was born. Lucky, lucky, Lord!

With all this in mind, I've always felt predestined to work with food. However, my mother didn't want me to be a one-trick pony, and with dyslexia in tow, my academic career was not looking too hot. Nevertheless, being the clever academic that she is, my mother bought me a food lexicon to "trick" me into reading more and learning how to write properly. Yet, for what I've lacked in reading and writing ability, I've compensated for by working harder to develop what I actually enjoy doing: cooking. Good try, Mom, but cooking still wins! So I'll take credit for all the good recipes, but you will have to thank the publisher for spelling and grammar.

When my mother realized we would not be forming a mother-daughter, super-scientist team in white lab coats, side by side in front of microscopes, and saving the world together anytime soon, the two of us brokered a peace treaty. I was excused from boring household chores in exchange for having dinner ready and on the table when she arrived home from work. She was blissfully ignorant of what this would actually entail. Rather than providing

nutritionally balanced meals, I was hell-bent on trying new culinary experiments. French chicken liver paté served with a slice of Schwartzwald cake for dinner—nothing was wrong with that in my book!

Much to my mom's dismay, I finished my academic pursuits at the tender age of 16, and went on to pursue a glamorous career in a café, feeling on top of the world! Who needs college when you can be a master chef trying to change the world one tart at a time? Right?

Wrong. I quickly realized that a pastry at a time is exactly that: one pastry. I aspired to become a chef, but as I found myself preparing the same dishes over and over again like some *I Love Lucy* marathon. The job of my dreams wasn't all that it was cracked up to be. I wanted creativity and all I got was cupcakes—again, and again, and again.

I felt like I was suffering from an early–onset midlife crisis and wondered if there was any other type of work within the food industry. It all hit me when I was at university *(Kids: Stay in school!),* where I discovered that there was a whole industry around events. From presentation and design to creative menu compositions, finally I had found the career for me. So upon graduation I hopped on the first Greyhound bus to New York and I have been here ever since.

For those first few years in the biz, those family recipes, with some additions of my own, provided a great foundation. This, combined with the classical skills from culinary school, helped me develop my own cooking style early.

So, to me there's no better way to introduce myself than by sharing my recipes: a little Americana, a dose of French from my Francophile grandmother thrown in there, and a large dollop of Scandinavian as well.

Collect your family's recipes and take good care of them. They say more about you than you think.

Bacon & Leek Quiche

The key to making a great quiche is the filling. Make sure to use ¼ cup of heavy cream and ¼ cup of milk per egg. That's it!

1 quiche; serves 6 to 8.

Pie dough (store-bought or refer to recipe for apricot pie, on p. 123)

1 leek

10 oz. smoked ham or bacon

1 tbsp. butter

10 oz. grated, aged cheese, such as Cheddar

Filling:

3 large eggs

2 cups milk

⅔ cup heavy cream

¼ tsp. cayenne pepper

Salt and freshly ground black pepper

1. Make the pie dough by following the instructions for apricot pie on page 123. Chop off the bottom of the leek, cut the leek in half length-wise, and slice it thinly. Place the sliced leek in a colander, and rinse thoroughly under running water.
2. Cube the ham or bacon and sauté it in a frying pan on medium heat until crispy. Remove from the pan and set it aside. Add butter to the pan, and sauté the leeks until translucent.
3. Preheat the oven to 350°F. Flour a clean counter top and roll out the pie dough. Place dough into a pie tin, and use a fork to press the dough up along the sides. Prick the dough at the bottom of the pan. Place the pie shell in the freezer for 5 to 10 minutes. This will help keep the crust in place once it is baked.
4. Time to assemble the quiche. Place the leek, bacon or ham, and half of the grated cheese into the bottom of the shell.
5. Whisk together the filling and pour it over the filled sheet. Sprinkle the top with the remaining grated cheese. Bake in the oven for about 40 minutes, or until the filling has set, no liquid shows when you jiggle it, and the surface is golden.

Ever thought of grinding your own hamburger meat? Well, you should. And this is how you do it.

A better burger – *Blend your way to a better burger.*

10 oz. beef per person; use cuts such as sirloin, short rib, chuck, skirt steak

---

Salt & freshly ground black pepper

The best burger sides:

- Brioche buns
- Dijon mustard
- Mayonnaise

1. Most cuts will do the job, but pick a nice cut of beef with good marbling. Cube the meat and place it in a heavy-duty blender with blades addition (personally, I use a Ninja mixer for this recipe) and a good pinch and salt and pepper. Using the pulse function, grind the meat about 20 pulses, or until it has the consistency of Steak Tartare. Loosely shape the meat into patties.

2. Cook 'em up like you normally would on the grill or in a cast iron skillet. Easy peasy, but better flavor is guaranteed. As a European, I of course recommend you serve them up with classic euro toppings such as Dijon mustard and mayo all piled on a on brioche bun. But hey, that's just me.

Cheesy
Cauliflower

1. Fill a large pot ⅔ full with water, and add a pinch of salt. Bring to a boil. Clean the cauliflower head by trimming off all the leaves and the bottom stem. When the water reaches a boil, add the cauliflower to the pot and let it cook for 7 minutes.
2. Chop the onion, garlic, and ham. Heat the butter in a deep skillet over medium heat and sauté the onion, garlic, and ham until the onions are translucent .
3. Add in the cream, bouillon cube, and cayenne pepper and let simmer down until it thickens, about 5 minutes or so. Add salt and pepper to taste.
4. Preheat the oven to 350°F. Butter an ovenproof dish, place the lightly cooked cauliflower in it, and spoon the sauce over the cauliflower head. Sprinkle the grated cheese on top. Bake for about 15 minutes or until the cheese has melted and is a golden brown.

1 head of cauliflower

1 yellow onion

2 garlic cloves

8 oz. smoked ham

1 tbsp. butter

1 cup heavy cream

¼ tsp. vegetable bouillon cube

¼ tsp. cayenne peppar

6 oz. grated hard cheese, such as Cheddar

Salt & black pepper

Simple Seafood *Skillet*

If there's one thing I can daydream about in New York, it's this dish with Norwegian lobster (or as we call it, langoustines).

15 langoustines; can be substituted with large-headed shrimp

———————————————————

5 oz. butter

———————————————————

3 garlic cloves, finely chopped

———————————————————

1 bunch of chives, finely chopped

———————————————————

½ cup dry white wine

Serves 4.

1. Preheat oven on its highest setting.
2. Mix the butter with the chopped garlic and chives. Cut the langoustines in half lengthwise, and remove the black vein and head. Place the langoustines, cut-side up, in a large, cast-iron skillet. Pour the wine and spread the garlic butter in a thick layer evenly over them.
3. Cook in the oven for 10 minutes. Change the oven setting to "broil" for the last few minutes.

Oven–Braised Cod *with* *Mushrooms &* *Tomatoes*

Serves 4.

1.5 lb. thick, cod fillets

7 oz. button mushrooms

2 tbsp. butter

½ cup dry white wine

1 cup heavy cream

½ vegetable bouillon cube

1 yellow onion

1 pint cherry tomatoes

Salt & ground white pepper

To serve:
Boiled potatoes

Vegetables

1. Clean, slice, and sauté the mushrooms in a skillet with a pat of butter until they're golden. Let rest.
2. Bring the wine, cream, and bouillon to a boil in a saucepan and let simmer on low heat until thickened, about 10 minutes.
3. Preheat the oven to 350°F. Butter an ovenproof dish and place the cod fillets in it. Season the fish with salt and pepper. Slice the onion, halve the tomatoes, and place them on the cod. Add the sautéed mushrooms, and pour the reduced cream and wine sauce on top.
4. Bake in the oven for about 20 minutes. Serve the cod with boiled potatoes and vegetables.

Tenderloin with Roasted Garlic Butter

I'll admit it: I can be a bit of a trend victim when it comes to the latest in food. But, hello? Whatever happened to delicious classics like the flank steak or chocolate mousse? Pressure to follow the latest and greatest food trends—I'm looking at you cupcakes and cronuts—has caused so many of our favorite go-to's to be forgotten—recipes just like this dish, which is crazy good and a total classic.

4 servings

1 beef tenderloin, approx. 2 lbs.
———————————————————————————
6 heads of garlic
(yes heads, not cloves)
———————————————————————————
7 oz. butter
———————————————————————————
¼ cup parsley, coarsely chopped
———————————————————————————
mixed fresh herbs, you can use what you have here
———————————————————————————
Salt & freshly ground pepper

1. Take a large piece of foil, about 15 inches in length and fold it in half. Break the garlic head into cloves and set them down in the middle of the foil. Dab about 3 tablespoons of butter onto the garlic and close the foil to make a parcel. Place the parcel on the grill at medium heat, or bake in the oven at 350°F. It will take about 20 minutes for the garlic cloves to soften. Once done, set aside and let cool.

2. Dry the tenderloin with paper towels. Pour a good amount of salt and pepper onto a cutting board, then roll the tenderloin in the seasoning.

3. Peel the cooled and roasted garlic cloves and place them in a bowl. Mash them roughly with a fork and mix with the butter. Chop the herbs and add them to the butter. Mix, then season with salt and pepper.

4. 2-step grilling: Light up the grill or heat up a cast-iron pan. Sear the tenderloin on high to give it a good, dark crust. Set the tenderloin in an ovenproof dish, then finish cooking by roasting it in the oven at 350°F for about 10 minutes.

5. To serve: Remove the tenderloin from the oven and set it on a piece of foil. Add the garlic butter on top, then close the foil around the meat. Let the meat rest and the roasted garlic butter melt for about 5 minutes before serving.

Chocolate Mousse

6 oz. dark chocolate
(65 – 70% cacao is best)

2 large eggs

⅓ cup granular sugar

1 cup heavy cream

½ tsp. vanilla extract

¼ tsp. salt

Serves 6 to 8.

These days, chocolate mousse is about as cool as Britney Spears and Crocs. After being a menu staple for almost a hundred years, the chocolate mousse has all but disappeared for no real reason that I can think of. It fucking rocks. *Bring back the mousse!*

TIP!
Try serving up your chocolate mousse with port wine or sherry.

1. Separate the egg whites from the yolks, and place them in separate bowls.
2. Bowl 1: With a mixer, beat the egg whites with the sugar until soft, meringue-like, peaks form.
3. Bowl 2: In a separate bowl, whip the cream with the vanilla extract.
4. Bowl 3: Break the chocolate into small pieces and melt it in the microwave or over a water bath. Remove from the heat and stir the chocolate with a spatula to cool. Fold in the yolks and the salt.
5. In a large bowl, use a spatula to fold in the contents of the three bowls by alternating between the three until they form a chocolate mousse. No stirring here, please, stick to folding. Let the mousse set in the fridge, for about 2 hours. Dig in.

At the Canary Islands in the early 1990s, the birds were chirping and the sun was shining, and I took a giant bite of the best thing I had ever seen: a banana split. "Mom, are there seeds in bananas?" I asked. We looked down into the banana and cream mixture, only to find something hard, white, and bloody. It wasn't the best start to my childhood infatuation with this ice cream treat—I had just lost my first tooth.

Foster's
Banana Split

Super easy and a whole new level of delicious. Simply heat the cream in a saucepan over low heat and add the chopped chocolate, then stir until it has melted and formed a chocolate sauce.

Serves 4.

1. Peel and cut the bananas lengthwise. Heat butter, sugar, and rum in a large skillet and let it cook to a caramel-like consistency for about 5 minutes. Add the bananas and let them caramelize in the caramel mixture, turning occasionally, for 2 minutes or until the bananas are soft.
2. Make the chocolate sauce (see the recipe).
3. Place the bananas in a bowl, or better yet, in a banana-split dish if you happen to have one. Drizzle the rum and sugar sauce from the skillet over the bananas. Scoop ice cream on top and drizzle chocolate sauce all over it. Yum!

4 bananas

3 tbsp. butter

¾ cup sugar

⅓ cup dark rum

Real Chocolate Sauce

5 oz. dark chocolate, chopped

½ cup heavy cream

Recipes for Aperitifs, *Cocktails & Parties*

Saturday night, the clock has just struck seven, and you're terrified of the cocktail party you've invited people to but have yet to do anything for. It's time to get your shit together. Are you afraid that both the local liquor store and your wallet will be drained in the process? Or maybe you're worried about all of the necessary ingredients, electrical gadgets, measuring sets, bar spoons, and those citrus peel thingamajigs that you definitely don't have? *Take it easy!*

We all enjoy a fancy-ass, professionally mixed cocktail, but when at home, don't try and emulate the bartenders that have learned so many tricks that they've earned their PhD in mixology. For us regular-joes that don't own a bar spoon or have a habit of burning orange zest on a regular basis, there are other solutions.

Honestly, who the fuck has the time to put together a whole sit-down dinner? A cocktail party is the easiest way to entertain your friends. It can be an evening-long event or a short happy hour where everyone can meet up before heading out for the night's main event. All you have to do is remember a few simple rules to make this a great night. The most important is to let your guests know in advance that this is a cocktail party, not a full-on feast, so they don't show up too hungry at your doorstep.

A cocktail party can be as complex or as simple as you want it to be. If you want to go all out with

a theme, attire, finger foods, napkin origami, ice sculptures and whatnot, then go for it! If not, make the night a laid-back get together with a few drinks and some simple snacks. How much time and money you spend on it is up to you.

But what is a cocktail party without a cocktail?

You don't need a fully stocked bar. It's perfectly fine to offer two or three premixed drinks to your friends. You can make and mix most drinks ahead of time and keep them in a big pitcher. As guests arrive, add ice and they'll be cooled down in a few minutes. You may not get the "Mixology Association's" seal of approval, but then again, who the hell cares as long as you and your friends can hit the sauce!

What you really need to throw a cocktail party

Which glass?
For a party it's totally okay to slim down your choice of glassware:

Cocktail glasses are used for all cocktails served *straight up**, i.e., chilled drinks that are served strained of their ice.

Lowballs or **rocks glasses** are used for drinks, such as whisky, served neat (without added water or ice) or "*on the rocks*" (with ice cubes).

Highballs are for mixed drinks served with ice, but can also be used for soda and beer.

Wine glasses are used to serve red or white wine, but also come in handy for frozen cocktails containing crushed ice.

Port wine glasses are used for port wine, liqueurs, or alcohols served *straight up**.

Champagne glasses, flutes, or coupes are of course for Champagne, sparkling wine, and champagne cocktails.

How many drinks should I prep?
My formula for a cocktail party is simple. 2 drinks per guest the first hour, and 1 drink per guest, per hour thereafter.

How much booze should I buy for the party?
One bottle of Champagne (750 ml) serves approximately 6 glasses. If it's only used for a toast, it will stretch to 8 glasses. One bottle of the hard stuff (aka vodka and the like, 1000 ml – 1L) will yield about

22 drinks. One bottle of wine (750 ml) pours about 5 glasses. At the dinner table, count on one bottle of wine for every 2 guests.

Traditionally at cocktail parties you served cocktails, but these days you expect wine to be at a cocktail party so have some.

Beer is a no-no at a traditional cocktail party, but again, these days no one really cares about rules like that so have some of this too.

Want fewer dishes?
Your answer is probably yes, so put a mark like a sticker or a string on your guests' glasses so they'll recognize it throughout the night. Might sound kind of Stepford Wife-ish, but it works every time.

Vintage bar
These days who has a fully stocked *Mad-Men-style* bar hanging around your place. You're all good with two or three different premixed drinks ready to pour and maybe some wine. However, if you feel the pressure from your drunk uncle to have a fully stocked bar, you'll need vodka, gin, rum, tequila, whisky, cognac/brandy, as well as a few liqueurs at a minimum.

Cocktail Party vs. Cocktail Hour
Cocktail Hour is just that: an hour before dinner or another activity, with a few snacks and drinks. A cocktail party usually runs 2 to 3 hours long, with a larger selection of drinks and snacks. Make sure to be concrete with your plans for the evening; if it is an hour, enforce it, if it's longer, then don't worry about it.

ICE it down!
Don't fuck with ice, it can really affect the flavor of a drink! If you're going to serve punch, chill it by freezing a block of ice and throwing it in a punch bowl (duh) or carafe. Your punch will stay cold longer, and you won't have watered down drinks because a block of ice takes more time to melt than cubes. Your guests will be enjoying cool, delicious drinks for several hours without you having to lift a finger.

Berry & Brandy *Slushy*

Strawberry syrup:

½ cup strawberries, rinsed and sliced

½ cup water

¼ cup sugar

For serving:

Ice

½ cup pear cognac, such as Xanté

½ cup freshly squeezed lemon juice

1. Place water, sugar, and berries in a saucepan, bring to a boil, and cook for a minute or so until the sugar melts.
2. Pour into a blender and mix to a syrup.

To serve:

1. Break ice cubes in a blender until finely crushed, kind of like snow.
2. Scoop the crushed ice into cones or glasses.
3. Pour equal parts of strawberry syrup, lemon juice, and Xanté over the ice.

Bloody Campari *Slushy*

Blood orange syrup:

½ cup blood orange juice
(bought or freshly squeezed)

½ cup sugar

½ cup blood orange, cut into slices

To serve:

Ice

½ cup Campari

1. Place water, sugar, and orange slices in a saucepan, bring to a boil, and cook for a minute or until the sugar melts.
2. Pour into a blender and mix to a syrup. Mix in the blood orange juice.

For serving:

1. Break ice cubes in a blender until finely crushed, kind of like snow.
2. Scoop the crushed ice into cones or glasses.
3. Pour equal parts of blood orange syrup and Campari over the ice.

All recipes serve 6 to 8 snow cones.

I ❤ COCKTAILS

'RazzCello *Slushy*

Raspberry syrup:

½ cup raspberries

½ cup water

½ cup sugar

For serving:

Ice

¼ cup freshly squeezed lemon juice

½ cup limoncello

Snow cone bar:

1. Using an ovenproof pan or a Tupperware container, freeze a large block of ice. It will take approximately 18 to 24 hours to harden.
2. When you're ready to serve, set up the bar by positioning the block of ice on a cutting board and decorating all around it, with halved lemons, for instance. Using an ice shaver (it looks like a wood planer; you can find it online for about $10), shave the ice into snow-like flakes.

1. Place water, sugar, and berries in a saucepan, bring to a boil, and cook for a minute or so until the sugar melts.
2. Pour into a blender and mix to a syrup.

For serving:

1. Break the ice cubes in a blender until finely crushed, kind of like snow.
2. Scoop the crushed ice into cones or glasses.
3. Pour equal parts of raspberry syrup, lemon juice, and limoncello over the ice.

Boozy *Latte*

Boozy latte works a bit like a liqueur and coffee in one. It's an excellent after-dinner drink.

4 cups brewed coffee

1 cup coffee liqueur

Ice

1 cup half-and-half

Nutmeg

1. Brew the coffee and pour it into a large pitcher. Leave it in the refrigerator to cool.
2. Before serving, add in the coffee liqueur and a handful or so of ice.
3. Whip the half-and-half quickly until frothy.
4. Pour the iced coffee in glasses, add a few spoonfuls of creamy froth, and top with some grated nutmeg.

One pitcher; serves 8.

Punchbowl 'Barb

The bitter liquor Aperol actually contains rhubarb and works well in an aperitif drink.

1 punch bowl, makes approximately 8 to 10 drinks.

6 rhubarb stalks

1 cup sugar

1 cup water

Aperol

1 bottle Champagne, Brut, or sparkling wine

1. Trim and cut the rhubarb into cubes, then place them in a saucepan with the sugar and water. Bring to a boil and let simmer until the rhubarb has softened, which takes about 15 minutes. Mash the rhubarb mixture with a fork.
2. Pour the rhubarb mixture into a large pitcher or punch bowl. Mix in an equal amount of Aperol and top it off with sparkling wine.

The idyllic US state of Vermont is home to the legendary Ben & Jerry's. As a child, I lived in Vermont for a few years, and I remember especially one day of the year all the children looked forward to. No, not Christmas Eve. We waited with childlike delight for the city's annual free cone day—a day when tho whole of Vermont got *free ice cream* and the yellow school buses took the kids to the Big Ben & Jerry's factory. In other words, I learned early to love ice cream and my favorite flavor was Cherry Garcia, which was what my mother always brought home.

2 scoops of Ben & Jerry's Cherry Garcia ice cream

¾ fl. oz. cherry liqueur

---

1. Blend the ice cream and liqueur; press the pulse button about 15 times.
2. Serve immediately in a glass with a straw.

Cherry Garcia
Boozeshake

Serves 1 milkshake.

Bourbon Sipping *Cream*

I first heard of "sipping cream" during a weekend in Nashville. I started chatting with a girl who mentioned that her grandmother made her own Bailey's Irish Cream, which she called *sipping cream*. What?! Homemade cream liqueur?! I never did get to taste the Tennessean's drink, but I had to try making it in my own kitchen as soon as I got back to New York.

Serves 10 to 12.

1¾ cup bourbon or whiskey

1 scant cup heavy cream

1¾ cup sweetened condensed milk

1 tbsp. instant coffee granules

2 tbsp. chocolate sauce

2 tbsp. vanilla extract

2 tbsp. powdered sugar (optional)

Ice

1. Blend all ingredients except the ice. Taste. If you prefer a sweeter drink, then add in 2 tablespoons of confectioner's sugar. The alcohol acts as a preserver for the cream, which allows this drink to stay fresh in refrigerator for at least 2 weeks.
2. Serve over ice as an after-dinner drink.

Hotty *Toddy*

1 quart apple juice, freshly pressed

¼ cup of mulling spices (or 3 whole cardamom pods, 1 cinnamon stick, 4 whole cloves, and dried orange peel)

1 tsp. butter

½ lemon, sliced

Brandy or whisky (optional)

1. Heat the apple juice and spices in a saucepan over low heat until it starts to simmer. Remove the pan from heat, add in the butter, and let it steep.
2. Serve with a slice of lemon. For an adults-only version of the drink, add in a shoot of brandy or whisky.

This drink works great either hot or cold. Simply add some ice for a cold drink.

Serves 5 to 6.

Flower Power *Punch*

It's back! My personal favorite has returned like an old ghost from the 1950s: the punch bowl. Power up your punch by freezing a block of ice with some edible flowers, herbs, candy, or fruit. Put a few candles out and you've got a great table decoration without even having to worry about flower arrangements.

¼ cup elderberry liqueur or syrup

3 tbsp. lavender flowers, fresh or dried

1 lemon

½ cup blackberries

1 bottle of sparkling wine, chilled

¼ cup of gin

1. Let the elderberry liqueur and the lavender flowers simmer over low heat for 2 minutes (losing the alcohol but gaining flavor). Let steep until it's cooled down and has absorbed the flavor of the flowers. Pass through a sieve to remove the flowers from the liquid.
2. Pour the elderberry and lavender syrup into a large glass bowl and add in the lemon juice. Place the blackberries in the bowl.
3. Right before the guests arrive: Top with sparkling wine, gin, and add the flowery ice cubes and a few extra slices of lemon. Place a large ladle in the punch bowl and let your guests serve themselves.

One punch bowl will serve 8 to 10 guests.

Flowering Ice Cubes

1. 1 bunch edible, pesticide-free flowers, such as lavender, nasturtium, violets, or roses.
2. Rinse the flowers. Place them inside the wells of an ice-cube tray, and fill the wells halfway up with water. Freeze the tray for about an hour.
3. Top the wells of the ice cube tray with more water and refreeze.

TIP!

Skip the cubes and freeze a larger block of ice in a container such as a large Tupperware. The block will keep your punch bowl icy cool much longer.

Punch Drunk

Tequila goes down easily mixed with watermelon. This drink is, in other words, a real party starter.

1 medium-sized watermelon

The juice of 10 lemons

1 cup agave syrup

3 ¼ cup tequila

1 handful basil leaves

Ice

One punch bowl will serve 25 to 30 guests.

1. Cut off the rind and the outer white parts of the melon and cut the red flesh into cubes. Make sure to remove all the seeds.
2. Place the melon cubes in a blender and purée—you might have to mix the cubes in several batches. Pour the purée into a pitcher or punch bowl.
3. Mix in the lemon juice, agave syrup, and tequila. Chop the basil and add it to the mix. Taste and adjust the flavor as needed. Right before the guests arrive, add ice to cool the drink down.

½ cup lime juice,
freshly squeezed

2 ¾ fl. oz. tequila

¾ fl. oz. Cointreau

¼ cup simple syrup

Approximately 10 ice cubes

2 bottles lager, Corona, or Sol,
for example

1. Pour lime juice, tequila,
   Cointreau, simple syrup, and
   the ice cubes into a blender.
   Blend thoroughly to make a
   Margarita-like drink.
2. Pour the beer into a large
   pitcher, add scoops of the
   frozen Margarita, and serve.

Lager-*ita*

Who would have ever thought
to put beer in a cocktail?
Apparently, a few people. It's
actually pretty good and works
wonders on hot summer nights.

Serves 4 to 5.

TIP!
This drink will get a smokier
flavor by substituting Mescal
for tequila.

Bloody *Rum*

1 cup dark rum, such as Zacapa
or Sailor Jerry

2 cups blood orange juice,
freshly squeezed

½ cup agave syrup

1 tsp. cinnamon, ground

Ice

1. Mix all ingredients, including
   the ice, in a small pitcher, strain
   into chilled cocktail glasses,
   and serve.

Makes 6 to 8 cocktails.

Lifesaver

Coconut water to the rescue again. It's the best way to avoid becoming dehydrated, a.k.a. the best way to avoid a massive hangover the next day. In one of my moments of sheer brilliance, the idea struck me: why not mix the coconut water right into the drink? Fight off that hangover before it even begins! Should work . . . right?

½ lemon, juiced

½ cup pisco

½ cup coconut water

1 cup limonata soda
(San Pellegrino Sparkling
Lemon, for example)

1. Pour pisco, lemon juice, coconut water, and limonata soda, along with a handful of ice, into a blender. Process until it reaches a slushy consistency.

Makes 2 drinks, or one coconut to share.

MEZZAN

Finger
Foods

Canapés, Bites & Snacks

A Monet painting was going to be auctioned off at Sotheby's. To celebrate the sale, Sotheby's had invited a select group of the world's top art collectors to celebrate. This occasion also happened to be one of the first events I planned on my own and I was fucking terrified. One by one, loaned Monet paintings, worth more money than I would ever see in my life, arrived at the auction house.

I was informed of Sotheby's strict, and at times slightly comical, rules and regulations. Apparently I was only allowed to serve white-colored food and drinks. Career-ending scenarios ran around in my mind like a dream sequence on the Food Network as I imagined food and drink right next to unfathomably expensive paintings. Considering there would be 25 guests all within prime spilling-distance of the paintings, I quickly hired the beefiest waiters I could find, hoping they could prevent any mishaps. Finally the night of the party arrived, and the guests of the evening, elegantly dressed in coattails and sequins, happily chowed down on that year's finger food *du jour:* risotto balls (all white, of course). Still, I'm not sure how much of the artwork they could actually see, since I had issued strict orders that there be a waiter stationed in front of every painting to prevent any of the revelers from getting too close. Fortunately, no Monets were harmed in the making of the event.

Welcome to New York in the 1980s:
Michael Douglas in *Wall Street*. Madonna wearing her cone-shaped bra. Yuppies talking on their brick-sized cell phones. Suddenly, fashion professionals who never had time to sit down to a proper dinner overran the town. Cocktail parties came back roaring harder than they had since the Prohibition era, and snooty French *hors d'oeuvres*, romantic Italian antipasti, sun-drenched Greek meze, and vodka-friendly Russian zakuski morphed into the finger food of choice for these events. Of course this trend exploded within the fashion industry, where everyone was waiting for a photo shoot or a runway show to begin and never had time for a full meal. Three-course-meals were replaced with large trays of small sandwiches, canapés, and the number one finger food of the eighties: the shrimp cocktail.

If you don't want to cook, just host a cocktail party! Whether you are serving canapés, *hors d'oeuvres*, finger foods, or cocktail foods, a cocktail party simply means you get to bring your friends together without having to worry about assembling a whole dinner. People mingle, the atmosphere is laid-back, and it's easy to put together a varied menu of finger foods, from light bites early in the evening to more substantial party fare later on at night. Get creative with your finger foods! And if your guests don't like your latest experiments, there will be another tray coming around shortly.

Sriracha
Popcorn

Serves 4 to 6.

1 bag unflavored,
microwaveable popcorn

¼ cup melted butter

3 tbsp. sriracha sauce

Salt

1. Pop the popcorn following the instructions on the packet. Melt the butter and mix in the sriracha sauce. In a large bowl or paper bag, shake the popcorn with the sriracha butter. Salt to taste.

Hot sauce, sriracha (or rooster sauce, as I call it due to the bird on the bottle), has a cult following these days; very few restaurants don't keep a jar of it on hand. Hot sauce is made by mixing, among other things, chili peppers and garlic, which are then left to age for several months.

Crispy
Almonds

Fills one 14 oz. bowl.

14 oz. almonds
—————————————————

Water
—————————————————

Salt
—————————————————

1 cup oil, for deep-frying
—————————————————

Sea salt

1. In a medium saucepan, bring salted water to a boil. Add the almonds and let them boil for about 2 minutes, until the skins starts to bubble.
2. Drain the water and rinse the almonds under cold water. Squeeze them between your fingers to remove the skins. Let dry on paper towels.
3. Heat the oil in a wok or deep sauté pan over medium heat. Fry the almonds for about 5 minutes, until they're golden but not brown (they'll taste burnt if they turn brown).
4. Remove the almonds from the hot oil with a slotted spoon. Coat them liberally with salt and serve.

Fried *Chickpeas*

1 14-oz. can of chickpeas

Peanut oil for frying

½ tsp. smoked paprika

Sea salt

Fills one small bowl.

1. Drain the chickpeas in a colander and rinse them well. Dry them thoroughly with paper towels. This will prevent the oil from splattering when you deep-fry them.
2. Fill a heavy, deep skillet with about ½ an inch of oil. Heat the oil on medium heat, do a test of the heat by adding one chickpea. If the oil bubbles around the chickpea and it becomes golden the oil is ready. Add the rest of the chickpeas and deep fry for about 5 minutes or until the chickpeas are a golden color. Stir gently occasionally and keep a lid handy in case of oil splatters.
3. Remove the chickpeas with a slotted spoon and let them drain on a sheet pan lined with paper towels.
4. When the chickpeas have cooled a little, transfer them to a bowl, and stir in salt and smoked paprika. Serve up.

TIP!
Chickpeas will keep for up to two days, so this snack can be prepared in advance.

Spicy Cheese Sticks

Store-bought frozen puff pastry is a lifesaver. You can use it to make a million things; one of my favorites are these spicy cheese straws.

1. Preheat the oven to 400°F.
2. Lightly flour a countertop and, using a rolling pin, roll out the defrosted puff pastry into 3 rectangles. Brush the bottom half of each rectangle with egg wash and sprinkle half the Parmesan cheese over it. Fold the top half over the bottom half and roll it out again.
3. Brush the rectangles with egg. Sprinkle poppy seeds on the first rectangle, cayenne pepper on the second, and the remaining Parmesan on the third.
4. Cut the dough into approximately ½-inch thick ribbons and place them on a baking sheet lined with parchment paper.
5. Press a fingertip onto the end of a ribbon and turn it gently into a spiral. Chill in the freezer for 15 minutes.
6. Bake the cheese straws for 12 to 15 minutes. After 5 minutes, turn the temperature of the oven down to 350°F. Turn the straws over once while baking to ensure they're evenly baked and golden. Let the straws cool on a rack before serving.

3 sheets of puff pastry, defrosted

Flour for the work surface

1 large egg, lightly beaten to egg wash

⅔ cup grated Parmesan

⅕ cup poppy seeds

2 tsp. cayenne pepper

Makes 18 to 20 cheese straws.

Surrounded by overly-tanned and overly-friendly Los Angelenos, the time had come for me to throw a party for KKK. Now before you scream to the internet and I become a trending story online, in LA, KKK stands for Kim, Kourtney, and Khloë Kardashian, the alliteratively-named sisters who have gained a stronghold on American pop culture. The party was held on a hotel roof and I was extremely excited because I had a big surprise in store for the guests. For one, the actor Elijah Wood—yes, Frodo Baggins!—was DJ'ing the party. But the big reveal came as Frodo got everyone into party mode. The lights dimmed and out came a team of synchronized swimmers dressed in 1950s swimwear as if they were Season One Mad Men rejects. They dove into the pool and performed a retro style, glamour-filled show. Everything went according to plan and I prayed that the Kardashian triumvirate had been impressed. At the end of the evening, I made my way over to the trio and asked them if they had enjoyed the party. They answered happily that yes, they had had a great time and their favorite part had been the pretty cocktails. Most of my efforts had been for naught, as the ladies had spent the entire night in the VIP lounge and had missed the show. Kardashians – 1, Linnéa – 0. Lucky for me, the drinks had been a hit!

Oyster *Shooters*

This recipe is a true classic. The shots will remind you of a Bloody Mary, but with an oyster in the middle. A perfect way to start the party!

1 cup tomato juice

2 tbsp. fresh horseradish, grated

1 tbsp. black pepper, coarsely ground

¼ cup vodka

½ lemon

Ice

4 oysters without the shell

1. Mix the tomato juice, horseradish, black pepper, and vodka in a pitcher. Squeeze in the juice of the ½ lemon, mix well, and add a handful of ice to keep everything chilled. Cut the other half of the lemon into smaller wedges.
2. Take 4 large shot glasses and place an oyster at the bottom of each one. Pour the tomato juice mix over it and serve the drinks with a slice of lemon wedged on the side of the glass. Now you're in business! Cheers!

Makes 4 shots.

Seafood *Dynamite*

Dynamite sauce:

½ cup aioli

1 to 3 tbsp. sriracha sauce

1 lime, juice only

Seafood skewers:

4 large shrimp

4 scallops

½ lemon, juice only

2 tbsp. olive oil

Salt & freshly ground pepper

The first time I ever had Dynamite sauce was while on vacation in Hawaii. The Japanese tourists were ordering the sauce day in and day out and that of course got me curious! Back in NYC I had to recreate the amazingness.

1. Skewer the shrimp and scallops.
2. Marinate in lemon juice, olive oil, and season with salt and pepper.
3. Mix the ingredients for the Dynamite sauce, adding sriracha to taste.
4. Grill the skewers for about 2 minutes on each side. Serve them smothered in the dynamite sauce.

Makes 4 skewers.

Lobster *Rolls*

As a seafood-loving Swede (as all Swedes pretty much are), a little part of me dies when the only seafood item on a menu is jumbo shrimp. Thankfully though, the lobster roll is always there to save me. I've eaten them in almost every corner of the Northeast, from Maine to Rhode Island. Luckily for me, and a few million other New Yorkers, the very best lobster rolls are right around the corner in the West Village at Mary's Fish Camp. Local lore has it that a foodie couple opened a restaurant, but when the relationship soured, Mary stormed out, leaving both her ex-girlfriend and the restaurant behind. But Mary, true to the spirit of outdoing one's ex, opened a new restaurant—Mary's Fish Camp—only one block away from her old place. Same menu, but the lobster rolls are way tastier. It's a revenge story tailor-made for a Lifetime movie.

2 lobsters, meat only

Approximately ½ cup mayonnaise

¼ cup chives, finely chopped

3 tbsp. extra finely chopped celery

1 tbsp. freshly squeezed lemon juice

Cayenne pepper

Salt & freshly ground pepper

For serving:

4 small rolls

2 tbsp. butter

1. Mix lobster meat, mayonnaise, chives, celery, and lemon juice. Taste and season with cayenne pepper, salt, and pepper.
2. Cut the edges of the rolls and fry them in a pan on both sides in butter.
3. Cut a slit in the middle of the warm rolls and add the lobster salad.

Makes 4 small lobster rolls.

Fancy Pigs
in a Blanket

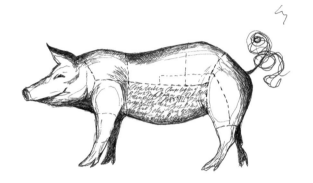

This is an upmarket version of the Stepford Wife all-time favorite.

15 smoked cocktail sausages

1 sheet of frozen puff pastry, defrosted

1 egg

⅕ cup poppy seeds

To serve:

Mustard

1. Preheat the oven to 400°F. Defrost the puff pastry and cut it into strips that are slightly narrower than the length of the sausages.
2. Roll the pastry strips around the sausages and pinch the dough to fasten it. The sausage is supposed to peak out from the pastry at each end.
3. Place the sausage rolls onto a baking sheet lined with parchment paper. Whip the egg lightly with a fork and brush each roll with the egg wash. Sprinkle poppy seeds on top. Bake in the oven for about 15 to 20 minutes or until the puff pastry has risen and is golden in color. Serve with mustard.

Makes 15 pigs in a blanket.

1 chicken breast

1 cup dry, white wine

The peel of ½ preserved lemon (or the finely grated peel from 1 lemon)

10 green olives, pitted

¼ cup mayonnaise (preferably made with olive oil)

1 tbsp. fresh or dry tarragon

Salt & freshly ground pepper

To serve:
Crisp bread sticks

Preserved Lemon
Chicken Salad

As a naïve 20-something working in New York kitchens, I quickly had to learn how to work with exotic ingredients I had never heard of before, one of them being Moroccan preserved lemons, which has now become one of my go-to ingredients.

1. In a large saucepan with a lid, cook the chicken breast in the white wine for about 15 minutes.
2. Remove the chicken breast from the pan and let it cool. Cut it into small cubes and place them in a bowl. Finely chop the preserved lemon peel, olives, and tarragon and mix with the chicken.
3. Stir in the mayonnaise and season with salt and pepper to taste.
4. Let stand for at least 30 minutes to let the flavors develop. Serve as a dip with crisp bread sticks.

Serves 6 to 8.

Moroccan Preserved *Lemons*

You can usually find preserved lemons at a Moroccan market or specialty store, or you can of course make your own if you have a few extra weeks to spare. In case you feel up for it, here is how it goes.

1. Squeeze the juice of 2 lemons. Wash the other 5 lemons thoroughly in warm water and cut four deep slits lengthwise into each washed lemon.
2. Fill the slits with salt and place the lemons in the jar, pressing down on the lemons slightly with a large wooden spoon to make some of their juice seep out. Using a jar that the lemons will fit into only if squeezed into, fill the jar. Cover the lemons fully with lemon juice and a layer of salt.
3. Place the jar in a dark and cool place. For the first week, open the jar every other day and press down on the lemons until they're covered in juice.
4. Let the lemons sit and cure in the jar until the peels become very soft, usually about 4 weeks. Rinse the lemons before using them. They work great with fish and chicken dishes.

7 organic lemons

Kosher salt

A large glass jar with lid

Eggplant *Pantesca*

1 ½ lb. eggplant

3 tbsp. salt

¼ cup almonds, marcona preferably

¼ cup green olives, pitted

7 oz. mozzarella cheese

10 basil leaves

¼ cup Parmesan cheese, grated

Freshly ground pepper

⅔ cup olive oil

Serves 8 to 10.

1. Slice the eggplant into half-inch slices.
2. Salt both sides of the slices and let them sit for 30 minutes to "sweat." Don't skip this step as it creates the flavor.
3. Using the 'broil' setting, preheat the oven to 450°F.
4. Chop the almonds, olives, mozzarella, and basil and mix it all with the grated Parmesan. Add pepper to taste.
5. Rinse the salt from the slices of eggplant and pat dry. Heat approximately 3 tbsp. olive oil in a skillet and sauté the eggplant until soft and both sides are golden. You will need to sauté in multiple batches, adding more olive oil to the pan as needed.
6. Sprinkle the slices of eggplant with pepper and place them on a baking sheet. Add the filling to the middle of the slices. Broil for 3 to 5 minutes or until the cheese has melted.

Hot
Cups

1 cup peaches, peeled and diced

1 cup watermelon, rind removed and flesh diced

1 cup cherry tomatoes, halved

1 handful fresh basil leaves

1 handful lemon balm leaves

¼ cup apricot preserves

3 tbsp. chopped jalapeños

Juice of ½ lemon

3 tbsp. olive oil

Salt & freshly ground pepper

1. Mix the peaches, watermelon, and tomato halves. Coarsely chop the basil leaves and lemon balm. Combine everything in a bowl.
2. Melt the apricot preserves in a small saucepan and stir in the chopped jalapeño. Let simmer on low heat for a minute.
3. Remove the preserves and jalapeño from the heat and stir in the lemon juice and olive oil. Add salt and pepper.
4. Mix the salad with the dressing. Serve in glasses with a spoon.

Serves 6 to 8.

Easy *Elotes*

(a.k.a. Mexican corn on the cob)

Contrary to popular belief, the state of New York isn't only comprised of the "Big Apple"—you only have to travel half an hour out of the city to find yourself deep in farm country. Luckily you can find a bit of this farm country in the heart of the city itself as every Monday, Wednesday, Friday, and Saturday, hipster farmers pull into Union Square and set up stalls for the Farmer's Market, where you can buy most any food grown or raised locally.

This recipe is inspired by a truly amazing Mexican street food called *elote*.

4 ears fresh corn

½ cup coconut flakes

Ancho chili and honey butter:

3½ oz. butter

1 tsp. smoky chili pepper
(such as ancho chili)

2 tbsp. honey

To serve:
1 lime

1. Set your oven on the broil setting.
2. Clean the corn by removing the innermost leaves. Pull the outer leaves back from the corn and use them as a handle.
3. Melt the butter and mix it with the ancho chili and the honey.
4. Broil or grill the ears of corn until they're soft, about 15 minutes, turning them frequently.
5. Toast the coconut flakes until golden brown in an oven set at 400°F.
6. Brush the corn with the butter mixture and sprinkle them with the toasted coconut flakes. Serve with a lime wedge.

Serves 4.

My Favorite
Recipes on a Stick

I love spearing food. In my office we used to say *Lollipop it*, but that was soon replaced by the short and sweet *Pop it!*. Regardless of what we call it though, food on a stick is a trend that's here to stay.

Granted, food a *la skewer* isn't always the most practical thing. It can be quite tricky to create something that looks amazing when it's perched on a super skinny stick. On the plus side, guests are pleasantly surprised by the fact that they no longer have to juggle their drink and a plate of food when trying to chat and shake hands with other guests. I have put a ton of different foods on a skewer during my time in the event biz—from pies, tacos, and popcorn balls, to frozen gazpacho for a warm summer's day.

Strawberry Schnapps Pops

TIP!
Boozy pops can be frozen in any mold. You can use anything from silicon molds to glasses and cupcake tins. Set them in the freezer for a few hours until the surface begins to freeze and then add in the stick.

1 lb. strawberries, rinsed and cut into wedges

4 tbsp. powdered sugar

1 tbsp. lemon juice

1¾ cups water

½ cup St Germain elderberry liqueur

Makes 10 to 14 Popsicle sticks.

1. Pour everything (except the popsicle sticks, of course) in a blender and process to a thin purée. Pour the purée into popsicle molds and freeze. Boozy pops will take slightly longer to freeze than regular pops—about 10 to 12 hours in the freezer.

Boozy Pops
Popsicle drinks are just what they sound like: drinks frozen into the shape of Popsicles.

Watermelon *Pops*

1 lb.+ seedless watermelon, cut into cubes

2 tbsp. powdered sugar

½ cup water

2 tbsp. lemon juice, freshly squeezed

2 basil leaves

½ cup gin

Makes 10 to 14 Popsicle sticks.

1. Pour everything (minus the sticks) into a blender and mix to a thin purée. Pour the purée into Popsicle molds and freeze. Boozy pops will take slightly longer to freeze than regular pops—about 10 to 12 hours in the freezer.

Sangria *Popsicles*

½ cup blackberries, fresh or frozen

½ cup raspberries, fresh or frozen

1¼ cup fruity red wine, such as Merlot, Cabernet, or Syrah

4 to 5 tbsp. powdered sugar
½ cup water

Makes 10 to 14 Popsicle sticks.

1. Pour everything into a blender and mix to a thin purée. Taste. Depending on the ripeness of the berries, more sugar might be needed. Pour into popsicle molds and freeze. Boozy pops will take slightly longer to freeze than regular pops – about 10 to 12 hours in the freezer.

Irish *Creamsicles*

½ cup Bailey's Irish Cream

1 ½ cup brewed coffee

½ cup half-and-half

Makes 10 to 14 Popsicle sticks.

1. Mix all the ingredients (minus the sticks) in a pitcher. Pour into Popsicle molds and set in the freezer to chill overnight.

TIP!
Serve your ice lolly drinks in a drinking glass with the stick up so guests do not have to spill on their clothes.

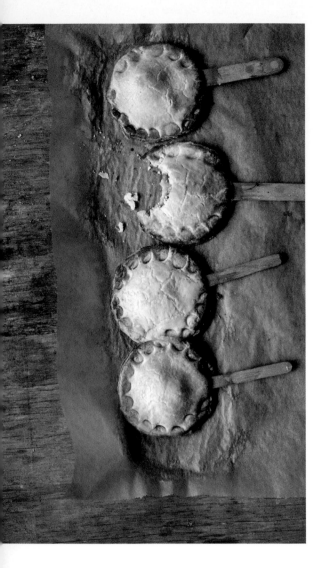

Pie *Pops*

First, cake pops took the world by storm. Now it's time for pie pops! Knowing the world we live in, no food is safe from being pop-ified.

Piecrust (store-bought, or follow the recipe on page 123)

---

6 Popsicle sticks

Filling:
¼ cup of your favorite jam
(raspberry or strawberry works well)

Topping:
1 egg

---

2 tbsp. raw sugar

Serves 6 clubs.

1. Preheat the oven to 375°F. Lightly flour a clean countertop and roll out the pie crust to approximately ¹⁄₁₀ inches in thickness. Using a wide-rimmed drinking glass (approximately 2.5 inches in diameter), cut out 12 circles. Sort of like making gingerbread cookies, collect the dough scraps several times, rework them into a new ball, roll it out again, and cut more circles.
2. Place 6 circles of dough on a baking sheet lined with parchment paper. Place a Popsicle stick across the middle of the circle and press down on it gently to make it stick to the dough. Place 1 tsp. of jam on the stick in the middle of the circle.
3. Cover each circle of dough with the remaining circles to make the lollipops. Press down along the edges of the dough with the handle of a spoon to seal the edges.
4. Beat the egg in a cup. Brush the pops with the egg wash. Sprinkle the pops with raw sugar.
5. Bake in the oven for about 8 to 10 minutes, or until the pops are golden and slightly puffy. Remove them from the oven, let them cool, and serve!

Tips!

What the hell IS a cocktail party anyway?

A cocktail party usually starts between 5 p.m. and 8 p.m. and lasts about 2 to 3 hours. Nowadays you can pretty much throw those rules out the window if you don't care much for formality. In other words, provide booze and food and people will show up, no mattor the hour.

Chair-Free Zone!

You know how standing desks became a thing? The same logic can be applied to cocktail parties. The whole point of hosting a cocktail party is to encourage guests to meet and mingle. Setting the party in a smaller space will spur people into starting conversations, as will removing most chairs from their immediate surroundings. A cocktail party is for mingling about and chatting. I figure on seating for about 10% of the company, others can stand or sit on armrests. Think intimate!

Hors d'oeuv . . . Uh, what?

Hors d'oeuvres is the French term for finger food, i.e. small foods that can be eaten in a bite or two. There are three classic forms of *hors d'oeuvres:* warm, cold, and canapés. What makes a canapé a canapé you might ask? Well, a canapé is a piece of food with a base, like a tiny open-faced sandwich. These names have since become passé and I generally refer to them simply as finger food.

Invitations!

An important detail when sending out invitations to a cocktail party is to let guests know that finger food will be served. That way you'll avoid confusing a horde of ravenous guests who think you'll be serving a feast.

Decorations! Decorations!

You can easily make decorative napkins by using a stamp or marker. It's far cheaper than buying store-bought party napkins. Just remember to use non-toxic ink—no ER visits at the party, please!

Napkins!

Get lots of small cocktail napkins for your party. Count on at least 4 per guest, as you'll also be serving foods on the napkins. Bonus: no dishes.

Tray trick!

One of my favorite tricks is to turn a picture frame into a serving tray. Buy a simple, inexpensive frame and then frame something that reflects the evening. Use decorative paper or fabric or even mint leaves and it instantly becomes a serving tray for drinks or food. For your next party you can simply reframe with something else that fits the event.

How much food?

My rule of thumb is to serve 5 to 6 different types of finger foods at a party, counting 1 or 2 pieces per guest, per recipe. Pair the food with a cocktail that is not too sweet, since the drink should complement the food. Wine is, of course, always a good choice.

Family
Style Dinners

Dinner Recipes that Let You Hang Out

"What's your best advice for throwing a great dinner party?" is something I hear as often as I hear a New Yorker complaining about the subway being late or the weather being crap—in other words, all the time!

The answer is pretty simple: chose something easy to cook and prep as much of the dinner as possible before your guests come over. Dinner at home should *not* be a carbon copy of a night out at a restaurant.

There's something tragicomic about how we all try to become the hostess with the mostest, as the Meryl Streep of the home, at each moment of the evening playing a different role. But let's face it, it's impossible to be a one-person restaurant. You just can't be the maître'd who greets everyone with a glass of champagne, the chef who cooks a stellar meal, and the waiter who artfully stacks his arms and tries to make it to the tables as fast as he can, all wrapped up in one. And of course this Meryl Streep-esque host must engage in light and witty banter with every guest and *somehow* pretend that their food is not burning in the kitchen while one guest tries to thank them, another apologizes for being late, and others ask when are we going to sit down and eat. Take a deep breath and relax! Everything might not be ready to go by the time your guests arrive and that's fine. Hand them a glass of vino and put them to work if you need some help. Forget about serving a three-course-meal, it's far too complicated. Make meals you can serve family style, put everything out at the same time, and tell your guests to have at it!

My first job in event planning was catering for my best friend's parents. I still don't understand how they dared to leave this task to a 15-year-old. They knew that I spent all my free time in the kitchen, but still. This was the equivalent of a kid who just learned how to swim being thrown in the deep end of a pool. I knew nothing about traditional party food, but what better way to learn than by experimenting?

Something possessed me to make the theme of the evening be flowerpots. Baked dinner rolls in flowerpots, roasted potatoes with sesame

and thyme in flowerpots, marinated olives in flowerpots, and dip and sauces in— *you guessed it*—flowerpots. Probably the only things not in flowerpots were the flowers themselves. The event was a rousing success, but I collapsed from exhaustion afterwards due to my own poor time-management. I had left all the prep to the last minute and everything needed to go into the oven at exactly the same time. It was a first-hand lesson in event organizing and I don't know if I can ever look at a flowerpot in the same way again.

Thankfully, with some time and experience, I got a bit better at managing my time and my menus. When I started to work in New York City, I had the opportunity to learn from some excellent French chefs, whose culinary expertise was overshadowed only by their outsized egos. They quickly put me in my place as the new kid in town. My first year in New York was spent as a trainee at one of the most revered event planning companies, where my colleagues guided me through the basics of event planning. The business was split into different departments for food, menu planning, design, flowers, mixology, wines, and service. The kitchen looked like it came straight out of a science fiction film. Despite my boss's *Français*, my time there was probably the best education I could have ever asked for.

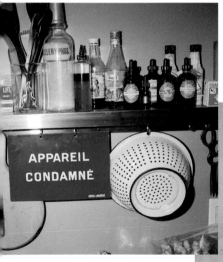

Wine–Stewed Beef *with Almonds*

1¼ lb. beef chuck, cubed

2 cups dry red wine

1 yellow onion

5 garlic cloves

1 pint cherry tomatoes

15 pearl onions

Olive oil

10 slices bacon

3 tbsp. butter

½ cup all-purpose flour

1 bay leaf

½ cup vegetable stock

1 tsp. smoked paprika

½ cup blanched almonds, preferably Spanish marconas

Salt & freshly ground pepper

For serving:
Loaf of bread

1. Place the beef chunks in a ziplock bag and pour the wine into it over the meat. Close the bag and let the beef marinate in the refrigerator for at least 2 hours, but preferably overnight.
2. Preheat the oven to 400°F. Slice the onion coarsely and place the garlic, tomatoes, pearl onions, and onion on a sheet pan. Drizzle with olive oil and sprinkle with salt. Roast the vegetables in the oven for 15–20 minutes, or until caramelized.
3. Chop the bacon and fry it until crispy in a Dutch oven or cast-iron pot. Remove the bacon and set it aside. Remove the pan from the heat and add 2 tablespoons of butter to the bacon fat.
4. Remove the beef from the marinade and dry it lightly with paper towels. On a plate, add the flour and salt and pepper. Roll the beef in the flour mix. Heat the Dutch oven with butter and bacon fat over medium heat. Add the beef to it and sear. Add the wine from the marinade and the oven-roasted vegetables and season with bay leaf, stock, and the paprika. Cover with a lid and let simmer over low heat for about 1 hour, or until the sauce has thickened and the meat is tender. Salt and pepper to taste.
5. Heat 1 tablespoon of butter in a skillet. Toast the almonds until they're golden brown. Add the bacon bits to the almonds and top the stew with the toasted almonds and bacon bits. Serve with fresh bread.

Serves 4.

Mozzarella-Stuffed *Meatballs*

1½ lb. ground beef

½ cup plain bread crumbs

1 tbsp. red pepper, dried and crushed

1 garlic clove

1 yellow onion

1 egg

3 tbsp. butter

½ tsp. salt

½ tsp. freshly ground pepper

Meatball filling:
8 small mozzarella balls, or one large cut into smaller cubes

½ cup Parmesan, grated

Oven-roasted tomato sauce:
(see the recipe on opposite page)

For serving:
Grated Parmesan

1. Mix salt, pepper, bread crumbs, and crushed red pepper in a small bowl and then set aside.
2. Peel the garlic and onion and grate them on a grater into a large bowl. Add ground beef, egg, and the bread crumb mix to the bowl. Mix and let rest in the refrigerator for 15 minutes.
3. Wash your hands. Remove the meatball mix from the refrigerator and divide it into 8 portions. Take one portion and flatten it in the palm of your hand. Place a mozzarella piece in the middle and sprinkle with 1 tablespoon of grated Parmesan. Close the meatball mix over the cheese and form a meatball. Do the same with the remaining portions.
4. Preheat the oven to 350°F. Melt 2 tablespoons of butter in a skillet. Sauté the meatballs on high heat lightly and carefully so they don't fall apart until they have a nicely browned surface.
5. Use the remaining butter to grease a deep, ovenproof pan and place the meatballs in the pan.
6. Pour homemade oven-roasted tomato sauce (see next page) over the meatballs and cook them in the oven for 20 minutes. Serve warm with extra Parmesan grated over the top.

Quick and Easy Oven-Roasted Tomato Sauce

2 pints cherry tomatoes

5 garlic cloves

1 yellow onion, thickly sliced

8 tbsp. olive oil

1 tbsp. sugar

1 cup of your favorite store-bought tomato sauce

½ vegetable bouillon cube

Salt & freshly ground pepper

This is my super quick and easy tomato sauce! If you're craving pasta or want to make a lasagna but don't happen to have a spare 4 hours or so to devote to tomato-sauce-making, just follow this recipe! Even though it only takes 30 minutes to make, it tastes like it's been simmering for hours. It's just as good with meatballs as it is on top of pasta.

1. Preheat the oven to 400°F. Place the tomatoes, garlic, and onion slices on a sheet pan. Drizzle with 2 tablespoons olive oil and season with salt and pepper.
2. Roast the vegetables in the oven for 15 – 20 minutes or until the garlic has softened and caramelized, shaking the baking sheet occasionally to prevent the tomatoes from sticking.
3. Peel the garlic. Pour 2 tablespoons olive oil into a skillet, heat over low heat, and add the garlic and the oven-roasted vegetables to it. Add sugar, tomato sauce, bouillon cube, salt, and pepper. Let simmer 5 minutes.

Serves 4.

This recipe started with a call I never in my life thought I would get. *Cosmopolitan* magazine was on the line and asked me if I wanted to cook with the boy-band and purity-ring famous Jonas Brothers. *Cosmopolitan* wanted to shoot Kevin Jonas (the eldest brother) and me preparing food together with his wife. Although I am by no means a teenager anymore or a Sunday school attendee, I couldn't resist and replied with an emphatic yes. Who turns down *Cosmo*? After a week emailing back and forth about the menu, I found myself at Kevin and Dani's house in New Jersey, along with a crew of 20 who shot my every chop and stir of the sauce. The day's result was a little cooking class and a dinner for the entire Jonas clan. As far as gossip goes, I can report that the family was extremely nice and very chatty and everyone loved these mozzarella-filled meatballs.

Hoisin–Barbecued
Pork Belly

Pork belly is the perfect party food, as it can be prepared well in advance and only needs a little reheating before serving.

1 lb. pork belly, with rind

¼ cup salt

water

Hoisin barbecue sauce:

1 cup hoisin barbecue sauce

⅔ cup honey

Freshly ground pepper

1. Cut slits in the rind in a close, checkered pattern. Salt liberally in the slits as well as all around the cut side. Place the pork belly in a ziplock bag and let it rest in the refrigerator, preferably overnight.
2. Preheat the oven to 400°F. Remove the pork from the refrigerator and wipe off all the salt with a paper towel. Place the pork belly, rind side up, on a rack set on top of a deep-rimmed baking sheet. Pour about 2 cups of water into the baking sheet. This will prevent the meat from smoking and the grease from splashing when it runs off the meat.
3. When you notice bubbles in the rind and it looks crisp, or after about 45 minutes, lower the oven temperature to 325°F and let the pork belly roast for another 1½ hours.
4. In a bowl, mix the hoisin sauce with honey and pepper. Cut the pork belly into thin slices and serve with the hoisin barbecue sauce.

Serves 4 to 5.

Warm Tomato Salad
with Burrata

1 burrata cheese, or 2 mozzarella cheeses

2 pints cherry tomatoes

15 pearl onions, or 2 large yellow onions, thickly sliced

2 bell peppers, red or yellow

2 tbsp. olive oil

Salt & freshly ground pepper

Dressing:

3 tbsp. balsamic vinegar

2 tbsp. honey

¼ cup olive oil

Coarse salt and freshly ground pepper

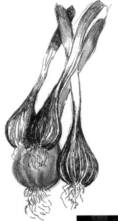

Burrata comes from Italy and it is one of my favorite cheeses. Imagine a more bougie version of mozzarella that is creamier and even better for melting on top of things.

1. Place the tomatoes on a sheet pan. Peel the pearl onions, slice the bell peppers, and place them on the baking sheet. Drizzle with olive oil and season liberally with salt and pepper.
2. Preheat the oven to 400°F. Roast the vegetables for about 20 minutes, or until they're soft and caramelized.
3. Mix all the ingredients for the dressing, whisking with a fork until it thickens.
4. Place the warm vegetables onto a large serving platter. Cut the burrata cheese into quarters and place it on the warm vegetables so it melts slightly.
5. Drizzle with the dressing and serve the salad warm.

Serves 4.

1½ lb. flank steak

---

15 pearl onions

⅓ cup olive oil

Juice of ½ lemon

½ cup herbs, fresh or frozen, chives, parsley, or marjoram works well

---

Salt & freshly ground pepper

Flank Steak
with Onion Chimichurri

1. Peel the pearl onions and place them with some olive oil on a sheet pan. Roast them at 400°F for about 20 minutes or until soft.
2. Season the flank steak with salt and pepper and heat the broiler, grill pan, or skillet until very hot. Grill the steak for about 4 minutes on each side so the surface is seared. Place the steak on the sheet pan with the pearl onions. Lower the oven's heat to 350°F and cook for 10 minutes.
3. Remove the baking sheet from the oven and tent the meat loosely with a sheet of foil while it rests. Put 10 of the pearl onions in a mixer and add olive oil, lemon juice, and the herbs, then mix until it becomes a pesto-like consistency. Season with salt and pepper.
4. Cut the flank steak into thin slices against the grain and drizzle with the chimichurri sauce. Garnish with the remaining onions.

Serves 2 to 3 people.

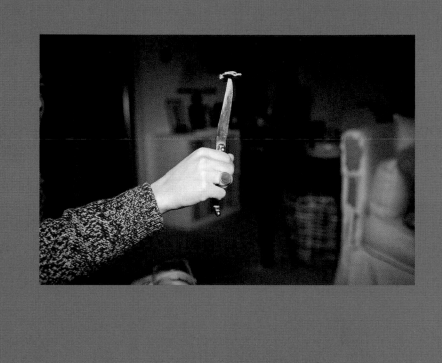

1 whole chicken

1 head garlic

3 small lady apples

1 lemon

5 prunes

5 sprigs thyme

1 tbsp. Calvados

3½ oz. butter

3 tbsp. mushroom soy sauce

1 tsp. pink peppercorns

1 cup heavy cream

Salt & freshly ground pepper

Oven–Roasted Chicken *with Calvados & Lady Apples*

1. Preheat the oven to 450°F. Rinse and pat the chicken dry with paper towels.
2. Separate the garlic cloves, slice the apples in half, and place them in a large, ovenproof pan.
3. Cut the lemon in half and rub the chicken with the lemon halves. Salt inside the cavity of the chicken. Stuff the lemon halves inside the cavity along with the prunes, sprigs of thyme, and Calvados.
4. Place the chicken in the center of the pan surrounded by the garlic and the apple halves.
5. Melt the butter and mix it with the mushroom soy sauce and pink peppercorns. Brush the chicken with this mixture and season liberally with salt and pepper.
6. Roast the chicken for 10 minutes or until the skin is lightly crispy. Brush on more of the butter mixture and lower the temperature to 400°F. Roast the chicken for another 40 minutes or until its juices run clear.
7. After removing from the oven, let the chicken rest for 5 minutes before serving. While resting, transfer the liquid from the bottom of the pan to a small saucepan and mix it with the cream. Bring to a boil and let it cook for a few minutes. Season with salt and pepper. Serve the chicken with the sauce.

Serves 3 to 4.

A Mini Wine Guide

I am no sommelier, yet I often find myself trying to pair wines with a new recipe that I've concocted. Thank goodness my mother—a physician by trade—has taken up a hobby in wine and oenology, the science of wine and winemaking, and has taught me a few tricks of the trade in the process. So thanks, mom, for drinking so much wine!

Again, I am no expert, but here are some simple rules I've followed throughout the years when pairing vino. In other words, a handy cheat sheet.

Champagne and dry sparkling wine usually work best when paired with salty snacks and finger foods.

Sauvignon Blanc is nice with dishes that have slightly acidic sauces or dressings. It's also good to pair with shellfish, fish, and milder cheeses, such as goat cheese.

Grüner Veltliner is excellent with dishes that are spiced with fresh herbs. This wine is slightly spicy so it works well with seafood, fish, and sometimes chicken, too.

Pinot Grigio is best served with light fish dishes, but it also works nicely as an aperitif.

Chardonnay: If the wine has been aged in oak barrels (such as those from southern Burgundy or California), it will be at its best when paired with fatty fish or seafood dishes in heavier sauces or poultry and other white meats. If not aged in oak barrels (like in the case of Chablis), it's better suited to lighter fish and seafood dishes.

Riesling goes best with sweet or spicy dishes, but Riesling also works with the same types of dishes that pair well with Chablis. While a semi-dry (with more sweetness), it nicely complements Asian dishes that have more heat.

Rosé: Some rosés are purely meant as an aperitif, but French rosé wines are excellent when served with different kinds of salads, chicken or seafood salads, for example.

Pinot noir: pairs well with dishes that have earthy flavors, such as mushrooms. It also works well with duck and other lighter meats.

Malbec can handle spicy dishes, as well as grilled lamb and beef.

Zinfandel is great with paté and terrines, but also pairs well with a hearty stew or grilled meat.

Cabernet Sauvignon is nine out of ten times the best choice for bloody beef. A dry 'Cab' also works well with game meats such as moose, venison, or boar.

Syrah is excellent when you serve up heavier fare. The wine itself is spicy and robust and its character is accentuated with the right combination of food and wine. A cream sauce will bring out the fruitiness in the Syrah. It can also be paired with game, lamb, or BBQ.

Are you still unsure of which wine to choose? Then follow this simple rule of thumb: buy wine that comes from the same region as the food that's on the menu. This is almost always a fail-safe.

Hazelnut & Parmesan *Kale*

2 bunches kale, coarsely chopped

---

1 cup hazelnuts

3½ oz. Parmesan

Salt

Dressing:

1 lemon, juiced

¼ cup olive oil

Salt & freshly ground pepper

1. Preheat the oven to 350°F. Chop the hazelnuts in half and toast them on a baking sheet until golden, about 20 minutes.
2. Mix the dressing and massage it into the kale so every leaf is well-covered. Let it sit for at least 20 minutes while the hazelnuts are roasting. Sprinkle with roasted hazelnuts and shave lots of Parmesan on top.

Serves 4 to 6.

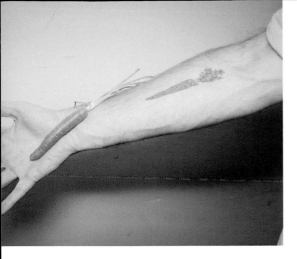

Oven-Roasted Carrots *with* Curry Oil & Fennel Seeds

2 bunches fresh carrots

3 tbsp. olive oil

2 tsp. curry powder

1 tbsp. fennel seeds

Salt & freshly ground pepper

1. Preheat the oven to 400°F. Mix oil, curry powder, and fennel seeds in a small bowl.
2. Wash and scrub the carrots and place on a sheet pan. Brush them with the oil mixture and season with salt and pepper.
3. Bake the carrots in the oven for about 20–25 minutes, or until the carrots have softened.

Serves 2 to 4.

Brussels Sprouts
with Balsamic & Mustard Seed glaze

1 bag Brussels sprouts, approximately 15 sprouts

⅛ cup olive oil

⅓ cup balsamic vinegar

⅛ cup yellow mustard seeds

⅛ cup honey

Salt & freshly ground pepper

Serves 4 to 5.

1. Preheat the oven to 375°F. Clean, cut off the stems, and half the Brussels sprouts. Place them on a rimmed baking sheet and drizzle with the olive oil. Season with salt and pepper. Bake for about 30 minutes, or until they've softened and started to brown.
2. Meanwhile, bring the balsamic vinegar, mustard seeds, and honey to a boil and cook on medium heat for 10 minutes. Remove from the heat and let sit until the sprouts are ready. Season with salt and pepper.
3. Place the sprouts in a bowl and toss with the dressing.

Roasted Whole *Garlic*

8 whole heads garlic

2 tbsp. kosher salt

3 tbsp. butter

½ cup olive oil

White bread, baguette or ciabatta

Serves 6 to 8.

1. Preheat the oven to 350°F. Cover the bottom of an ovenproof dish with kosher salt. Place the heads of garlic on the salt and dot each head with butter.
2. Bake the garlic for about 25 minutes, or until it has softened. Remove the dish from the oven and drizzle the garlic with the olive oil. Serve with bread.

Spicy Braided *Loaves*

Filling:

3½ oz. butter,
at room temperature

⅔ cup poppy seeds

3 tbsp. onion powder

1 bunch chives, chopped

⅔ cup Parmesan, grated

1 tsp. cayenne pepper

2 tsp. salt

2 tsp. pepper

Dough:

1¾ oz. fresh yeast or one packet
of dried yeast

¼ cup honey

1 tsp. salt

2 cups lukewarm water

2 lbs. all-purpose flour

1. Start with the filling: Mix the butter with the rest of the ingredients and let sit at room temperature.
2. Using a mixer with a dough hook, mix the yeast into the tepid water. Add in the honey and the salt.
3. Mix for about 3 to 4 minutes until all the honey, salt, and yeast has dissolved. With the mixer still running, add the flour, a bit at a time, until you have a loose dough. Let the machine go for another 10 minutes, adding more flour until the dough forms a ball around the dough hook.
4. Remove the dough from the hook and let it rise under a clean dishtowel for about 30 minutes, or until it has doubled in size. Place the dough on a clean, lightly floured work surface and knead it lightly. Cut the dough into 6 equal parts. Shape these parts to make 6 long rolls of dough and with a rolling pin flatten them completely. Spread the filling over the flat pieces.
5. Take 3 of the pieces, pinch them together at one end, and braid them into one long braid. Do the same with the other 3 pieces so you have two braided loaves.
6. Place the loaves on a baking sheet lined with parchment paper and let them rise for 45 minutes under a dishtowel.
7. Preheat the oven to 425°F. Bake the loaves on the middle rack of the oven and lower the temperature to 350°F after 10 minutes. Bake for 30 minutes longer, or until the loaves have a nice brown crust and they make a hollow sound when you tap on the bottom.

Makes 2 loaves.

Spicy Peach *Chutney*

3 peaches cut into approximately 1-inch large pieces

---

2 tbsp. butter

---

1 red onion, thickly sliced

---

2 garlic cloves, chopped

---

4 tbsp. mustard seeds

½ cup honey

¼ cup sugar

---

2 tbsp. chili flakes or ½ fresh chili pepper

¼ vegetable boullion cube

---

1 cup dry white wine

---

3 tbsp. balsamic vinegar

Salt & freshly ground pepper

Making your own sauces and chutneys is much simpler than you might think and they're a lot tastier than their bottled counterparts. This recipe serves 4 to 6.

1. Melt the butter in a deep skillet and add in the peaches, onion, and garlic. Sauté lightly and add the remaining ingredients except for the balsamic vinegar. Let simmer on low heat for about 15-20 minutes, or until the peaches 'fall apart' and the sauce has reduced. Season with salt and pepper. Add the balsamic vinegar and cook for 2 more minutes.

TIP!

Plums, apricots, or peaches work for this chutney recipe. Chutney will keep for about 1 week in the refrigerator and tastes great as is or you can make a quick sauce with them by mixing with an equal amount of crème fraîche. Serve it up with chicken or salmon.

Homemade Butter *in 10 Minutes Flat*

2½ cups room temperature heavy cream

---

2 tbsp. sea salt

1. Whip the cream with a mixer for approximately 10 minutes, or until it has separated into whey and butter. Strain off the whey and mix the butter with salt. The butter will keep in the refrigerator for about a week.
2. Serve with bread, cheese platter, or, for example, try it with radishes.

Tips!

Do the dishes, catering style!

If your party is a large one, take a tip from the pros and plan out your dishes catering style. Nothing stresses a host out more than an ever-growing mountain of plates and dirty dishes in the kitchen. It's pretty simple really. Block off an area, like in the garage, set up a garbage can, a slop bucket, and a basin with soapy water. Then scrape the worst of the leftovers in the can and place your dishes to soak in the basin overnight while you enjoy your party.

Not enough room in the fridge?

When cooking up a feast, your refrigerator has a tendency to overflow with wines that are chilling, sauces that are cooling, and so on and so forth. A tip I've picked up is to pack the washing machine with ice and place the bottles of wine, soda and beer in there—they'll stay chilled a surprisingly long time. You don't have to worry about ice melting as there's built-in drainage. If you don't have easy access to a washing machine, however, you can always make a good old ice bath. Fill a large basin one quarter full with ice, another quarter full with water mixed with a pinch of salt, and store the bottles in it. Everything will cool down in about 30 minutes.

Keep it seasonal!

Chefs love to talk up seasonal menus and I'm no different. Plan your menu with seasonal produce in mind and it'll be both cheaper and tastier.

Skip the ice!

This might be a bit OCD but there are a few things when serving wine that really bug me. Remember this:

1. Serve a glass of water with the wine, but skip the ice! Ice numbs the taste buds slightly so you might miss some of the flavors in the wine!
2. Don't fill a wine glass more than two-thirds of the way full. This is not some old-fashioned etiquette. It lets the wine stay at a steady temperature while being drunk and prevents it from warming up too much.

The Wine Myth!

I followed that little rule for a long time until an outspoken and offended sommelier attending one of my events promptly informed me that my wine was musty and warm. *Oh, the shame!*

Red wine should be served cool at 55 to 65°F, so if it's a hot summer day stick in in the fridge for a bit. While white wine should be served between 45 and 55°F—which was probably considered "room temperature" back in the day when this rule was invented.

Boxed Wine: Yay or Nay?

I shamelessly admit that I often serve boxed wine, since these days it's actually gotten pretty darn good. But I happily hide the box in the refrigerator, pour the wine into a carafe, and label it *'Cab', 'Red Zin', 'Grüner', or just 'Cheap Red'*.

How Much Food Should I Buy?

If you're serving a buffet or a large dinner, guesstimate just under a pound per person. Usually I split it up like this: 6 ounces of meat/fish/poultry; 5 ounces of vegetables; and 5 ounces of rice or potatoes.

As soon as I think of a three-course dinner

For some reason Beethoven's 5th symphony starts playing in my head. But even though I hardly ever cook a multi-course meal for my friends, there are times when you just have to do it. If you invite your mother-in-law over for dinner, she might give you some serious side-eye if you serve her mozzarella sticks and drinks in place of dinner, unless your mother-in-law wears ripped jeans, horn-rimmed glasses, and has lived in Brooklyn since before it was "cool," that is.

Cool moms aside, there are times when you should probably just set out the fine china and serve that cheese platter. For those occasions I suggest the following menu:

Menu

Starter: Champagne & Oyster Bouillabaisse
Entrée: Oven-Roasted Rack of Veal, with Lemon Gremolata
Dessert: Brandy Apricot Pie (From the Dessert chapter—see recipe on page 123)

Recipes for *thooose* occasions

This appetizer may seem a bit involved and over the top, but it's not that hard to make. In fact, this is one of those "use what you got because you are probably too lazy to go grocery shopping today" recipes. Granted, you might not have mussels just hanging out in your pantry, but they're not too hard to get. If you really want to suck up to your mother-in-law, substitute in some oysters.

Champagne & Oyster *Bouillabaisse*

1 cooked lobster, fresh or frozen

1 net oysters or mussels

1 lb. cod

3 tbsp. butter

2 yellow onions

4 stalks celery

2 garlic cloves

1 carrot

¼ cup parsley, chopped (including stems)

4 white peppercorns

¼ cup cognac

1 cup of water

2 cups dry sparkling wine or Champagne

1 vegetable bouillon cube

1¼ cup heavy cream

½ tsp. cayenne pepper

Salt & freshly ground pepper

1 bunch chives

3½ oz. sugar snap peas

1. Step 1: lobster stock. Preheat the oven to 450°F. Crack the lobster's shell and extract the meat inside. Place it in a bowl and refrigerate. Melt one tablespoon of butter in a large cast-iron Dutch oven or pot and sauté the lobster shell along with one onion, chopped coarsely. Place this mixture on a sheet pan and put in the oven for 20 minutes.
2. Chop the celery, garlic, carrot, and parsley. Melt one tablespoon of butter in the pot and sauté the vegetables for 2 minutes. Add the roasted lobster shell back to the pot, along with the white pepper. Pour in 3 tablespoons of cognac, the water, 1 cup of Champagne, and the vegetable bouillon cube. Bring to a boil and simmer for 20 minutes. Pour the contents of the pot through a fine-mesh sieve and use the broth as the base for your stew.
3. Bring your lobster broth and the cream to a boil. Add the remaining cognac and cayenne pepper. Let simmer and thicken for 15 minutes over low heat. Salt and pepper to taste.
4. Peel and slice the second onion, add it to the broth, and let it simmer for 10 minutes.
5. Meanwhile, scrub the mussels and place them in an ice–cold water bath. The ones that stay shut are alive. Add them to the stew. The open mussels, however, you can throw out.
6. Cut the fish into large chunks and add them to the stew. Chop half of the chives and add them to the broth. Simmer for 5 minutes. Add in the sugar snap peas, the mussels, and simmer for 2 to 3 minutes, or until the mussels start to open. If a mussel doesn't open once cooked, discard it. Add in the remaining chives, the lobster meat, and the last of the Champagne. Season with salt and pepper. Serve.

Serves 4 to 6.

Roasted Veal Rack
with Preserved Lemon Gremolata

One 4-chop rack veal

15 – 20 small new potatoes

1¾ oz. butter, melted

Salt & freshly ground pepper

TIP!
The recipe for Moroccan preserved lemons can be found on page 65. If you don't happen to have any preserved lemons you can also use regular, organic lemons. Just rinse them thoroughly in warm water before using them.

1. Preheat the oven to 450°F. Scrub the potatoes and place them on a sheet pan. Place the veal chops on the baking sheet with the potatoes. Brush the chops and the potatoes with the melted butter and season liberally with salt and pepper.
2. Roast the potatoes and veal rack for about 15 minutes, or until the rack has browned nicely. Lower the temperature to 350°F and continue roasting for 20 to 30 minutes. You can use a meat thermometer in the middle of the rack if you want to get a certain temperature on your meat.
3. Remove the rack from the oven and tent it loosely with foil. Let it rest for 10 minutes. Serve with the preserved lemon gremolata.

Top the veal rack with a spoon of gremolata and serve the rest from a bowl at the table.

Serves 4.

Gremolata:

1 lemon, the peel of one organic lemon, or one preserved lemon

1 bunch parsley

3 tbsp. butter

1 tbsp. sea salt

1. Peel the lemon, taking care to avoid the pith (the white part). Place it in a food processor with blades. Add the parsley leaves and pulse.
2. Remove the lemon and parsley mix from the processor and stir in the butter and salt by hand.

Sweets

Desserts, Cakes & Other Sweets

I have a nervous tic whenever something is bothering me or I'm stressed out: I run straight to my kitchen. First I open my refrigerator and then my freezer. Then I switch gears and put my nose in the pantry, all concentrated on figuring out something to cook or to bake to calm me down. Stress-eating in all its glory, I prefer to put a measuring cup in my hand and start baking to shift focus. A Princess Cake for when Sweden feels too far away; cupcakes to mend a broken heart . . . or that time when I baked the shit out of my KitchenAid mixer when a woman threatened to sue me after she swallowed a skewer at a party.

It was one of these times, too, that brought my Hurricane Chocolate Cake to life. Between progressively shorter commercial breaks, the TV was blaring the news of Hurricane Sandy's imminent landfall in New York.

With a knot in my stomach, I left Whole Foods $500 poorer—I don't know if that was because of the impending mega-storm or the fact that I willingly spent $500 at Whole Foods. After hauling ten fully-loaded grocery bags home, I confronted the very real possibility that my neighborhood might suddenly turn into Medieval Venice after the coming storm. Like a court chef preparing for a feast, I made enough food to feed an entire Palazzo. I started by roasting three chickens, each one with different seasonings. I whipped up a large bowl of pasta salad and assembled a rice salad with bacon. In between all of that and making peach chutney, I ran to the bathroom and filled the bathtub with water. A.k.a., I put together everything I thought we would need in case we lost power. Frantically, I told my boyfriend that I had to buy batteries on the black market since they were completely sold out in stores.

*Sweets for
my sweet,
Sugar for
my honey.*

With eyebrows slightly raised, he carefully made his way past the activity in the kitchen and into the living room, where he immediately tripped over the mini porta-potty I had bought in a moment of hurricane clarity.

The electricity did go out and naturally, because people expect that a chef in a disaster zone might be some combination of Mother Theresa and Julia Child, friends invited themselves over while everything else had shut down. We picnicked on the living room floor and ate chocolate cake by candlelight. Comfort food has never been so fitting a phrase.

Hurricane
Chocolate Cake

A good chocolate cake is the culinary equivalent of the *little black dress*. It's always there, it will never fail you, and no one will ever complain about it. It's your safety net when you're out of fresh ideas, but the party is still on and you have to pull your shit together. And anyway, who doesn't love chocolate cake?

8 oz. dark chocolate, preferably 60% cacao

8 oz. butter

½ cup all-purpose flour

2 eggs

1 cup sugar

1 tsp. baking powder

2 tsp. salt

1. Preheat the oven to 350°F.
2. Butter and flour a round cake pan.
3. Beat eggs and sugar until light and airy. Mix flour, baking powder, and salt in a separate bowl. Melt the chocolate and butter over a water bath or in the microwave.
4. Stir some of the flour mixture into the egg mixture and then stir some of the chocolate/butter mix into the egg mixture. Stir gently with spatula to keep the texture light and fluffy. Keep alternating the flour and the chocolate/butter mix until all of it is incorporated into the egg batter.
5. Pour the batter into the prepared pan. Bake for 5 minutes on the middle rack of the oven. Lower the heat to 300°F and bake for another 15 to 20 minutes. The cake should still be a bit gooey in the middle and the center of the cake jiggles if you shake the pan.
6. Put it in the freezer for a few hours. This will keep the cake's ultimate gooeyness for much longer.

The cake can be frozen for up to 1 month.

Makes 1 cake; serves 6 to 8.

Homemade *Peanut Butter Cups*

There is a God and he is the confectioner who decided to put peanut butter and chocolate together to create Peanut Butter Cups. Try this stupidly simple homemade version with dark chocolate and sea salt. *It's fucking fantastic!*

1. Set the molds on a baking sheet. If the paper is very thin, double up the wrappers.
2. Break the chocolate into small pieces in a glass bowl. Melt it either in the microwave or over a water bath, stirring often to avoid burning the chocolate.
3. Using two small teaspoons, cover the bottom and the sides of the molds with chocolate. Set the remaining chocolate aside for later. Put the cups in the freezer for about 10 to 15 minutes to make the chocolate set quickly.
4. Mix the peanut butter and 1 teaspoon of the salt. Remove the chocolate molds from the freezer and gently tap about 1 teaspoon of peanut butter into each wrapper. Do not fill each wrapper up to the top.
5. Gently reheat the remaining melted chocolate if needed and cover the peanut butter cups with a top layer of chocolate. Sprinkle with some salt and place in the refrigerator to set. The cups will keep about 10 days.

9 oz. dark chocolate, preferably around 65% cacao

½ cup chunky peanut butter, the best quality you can find

2 tsp. sea salt

Mini paper cupcake wrappers

Makes 10 to 12 peanut butter cups.

Boozy *Cupcakes*

Booze it up!*

Pretty much any dessert tastes better with booze. I dare you to prove me wrong on this one. Now, these desserts won't have you reaching for the aspirin in the morning—they're not that boozy—but they sure as hell are great. Willy Wonka said it best: *"Candy is dandy, but liquor is quicker!"*

4 vanilla muffins, homemade or store-bought

Frosting:

3½ oz. butter, room temperature

1 tsp. vanilla extract

⅔ cup powdered sugar

2 tbsp. espresso powder

1 tbsp. warm water

1½ tbsp. chocolate liqueur

1. With an electric or hand mixer, beat butter, vanilla extract, and powdered sugar until light and airy.
2. Mix the espresso powder in the water and stir well. Pour the coffee into the butter and sugar and mix well.
3. Using a thin piping nozzle, pipe some liqueur into the cupcake's center from the underside. Work slowly to allow the cake to absorb the liquid. Keep the muffins in their molds and decorate their tops with frosting. Place the cupcakes in the refrigerator for a bit before serving.

Makes 4 cupcakes.

Boozy Doughnuts with Crème Brûlée Topping

Nobody ever said that cooking on live television was glamorous. I was invited to *The Today Show* to make a boozy doughnut on their food segment with none other than Hoda Kotb and Kathy Lee Gifford. We stood side-by-side as I slowly began to fill a doughnut with what looked like a giant syringe. Kathy, naturally excited by the idea of a boozy doughnut, grabbed hold of a syringe and a doughnut and went to town. The doughnut erupted like a geyser. And Kathy was covered in sticky liqueur. Oh the shame! For a nanosecond I wondered if I'd got myself permanently banned from the show. However, being the pro that she is, Kathy laughed it off and went on to her next doughnut. I mean, what else would you expect from the woman who has nicknamed the days of the week 'Boozeday' and 'Winesday' on her fourth hour of *The Today Show*?

4 doughnuts, either homemade or store-bought

½ cup sugar

2 tbsp. coffee liqueur

TIP!
I doubt you own a kitchen-grade propane torch so try your oven's broiler setting to melt the sugar instead.

1. Preheat the oven to 250°F and warm the doughnuts for about 10 minutes.
2. Pour the sugar onto a plate. Brush one side of the doughnuts lightly with water and then dip them in the sugar to make a layer.
3. Using a small nozzle, pipe in the liqueur in several places on the doughnut's underside.
4. Burn the layer of sugar with a kitchen torch, or under the broiler, until the sugar makes a hard crust like creme brûlée. Serve up warm!

Makes 4 doughnuts.

Fashion Screams for Ice Cream

New York's *Fashion Week* in September marks the great return of those who make a biblical exodus every year to escape the city's heat waves. As soon as the fall 'season' begins, America's fashion Mecca is flooded once again and the onslaught of events begins. Rail-thin models bump heads with irritated publicists, immaculately dressed fashionistas, and celebrities from all corners of the world. You would think that for all these people who look like they don't eat that restaurants around the city would be empty, but you can never find a table at this time of the year.

For many years my job was to organize events for the fashion industry and the muggy tents at Fashion Week were the eye of the storm. Yet, for all the exterior glamour of the model- and celebrity-packed events, it's an absolute shit-storm behind the scenes. The pristine image of the events gives way to controlled chaos and performance anxiety, where models, designers, and fashion stars have less than 10 minutes to make an unforgettable impression on the crowd. It's a tall order!

After doing this for some years, the endless number of hungry, beanstalk women running around looking for low-calorie snacks led me to an epiphany. Cookies. Tell me one person on this earth who does not love a freshly baked cookie. Six months passed and when the next fashion week came around, I rolled my mobile oven into the tent and began baking warm cookies and served them with rum raisin ice cream. The irresistible smell of fresh cookies spread through the tent and a swarm of hungry Fashionistas came running at me like a high school track team. I could hear them muttering curses under every breath in true New York fashion as they took animalistic delight in the ice cream sandwiches.

Rum–Raisin
Ice Cream Sandwiches

⅛ cup rum, dark and spiced

¼ cup raisins

2 cups vanilla ice cream

8 oatmeal cookies (or whatever your favorite cookie is)

1. Mix the raisins into the rum and let them steep for about 1 hour, or until the raisins have absorbed most of the rum.
2. In a mixer with whisk attachment, mix the rum-soaked raisins with the vanilla ice cream. Put it back in the freezer, preferably overnight.
3. Slather the ice cream onto 4 cookies. Top the ice cream with the remaining cookies to make sandwiches. Serve immediately!

Makes 4 ice cream sandwiches.

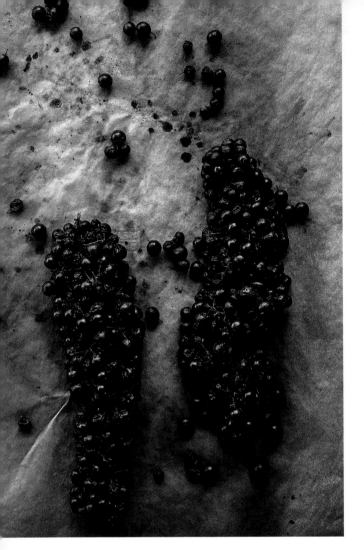

Make Your Own *Raisins*

2 bunches small, organic grapes

_____

Have you ever thought of making your own raisins? Probably not. Well, do it!

When you buy grapes, grab the smallest ones you can find. It will make the process a lot quicker. Make sure to leave the grapes in their bunches.

1. Preheat the oven to its lowest possible temperature, 150 to 200°F. Place the grapes on a baking sheet and let them dry in the oven. Check on the grapes periodically so they don't burn and flip them once or twice. The length of time it will take for them to dry will depend on their size, but count on about 2 to 3 hours.

Coconut *Baked Alaska*

The dish, named after Sarah Palin's home state, is just as simple as she is. In other words, it's fairly easy to make. Yet your guests will think you spent hours slaving away in the kitchen over this dessert. That couldn't be further from the truth—it's a piece of cake to make! (I hope you're thoroughly enjoying the bad dessert puns.)

1. This is by far the trickiest part of the recipe. The first step is to crack open the coconuts. Wrap each coconut in an old towel to get a good grip on it. Using a short, sturdy knife—a Swiss army knife or the knife attachment on a corkscrew will do the job—strike the knife with the hammer in several spots around the middle of the coconut until it splits in half. Watch your fingers! Pour out or drink the coconut water and put the coconut halves in the freezer. Repeat the process with the second coconut so you have a total of 4 halves.

2. Make the filling using a mixer. Beat the raspberries, sorbet, and liqueur quickly. Remove the coconut halves from the freezer and fill them with the sorbet mixture. Put them back in the freezer immediately and let them set for at least 2 hours.

3. With a mixer, beat the egg whites and sugar to make a meringue. It will take about 7 to 10 minutes to get white and fluffy. Once the mix has stiff peaks, it's ready to go.

4. Remove the coconut halves from the freezer. Spoon the meringue on top of the coconut halves. Brown the meringue quickly with a kitchen torch or on the broil setting of your oven for about 2 minutes, or until the meringue is golden. Serve at once!

Serves 4.

2 coconuts

1 hammer (yep, trust me, you'll need it)

Filling:

1½ cup raspberry sorbet

½ cup raspberries, fresh or thawed

¼ cup elderberry liqueur, such as St. Germain

Meringue:

3 large egg whites

1 cup sugar

Lady *Cake*

4½ oz. butter

1 cup sugar

2 eggs

1 cup all-purpose flour

⅔ cup almond flour

½ tsp. baking powder

Filling:
6 – 8 fresh figs

2 tbsp. sugar

Juice of ½ lemon

Glaze:
2 oz. butter

⅛ cup dark rum

½–¾ cup powdered sugar

I call this my Lady Cake. With the whole rum and fig thing, it gets a bit fancy, lady-like.

Makes 1 cake; serves 6 to 8.

1. Preheat the oven to 350°F.
2. Start with the cake: Melt the butter and let it cool. With a mixer, beat the butter, sugar, and eggs until light and airy. Mix all-purpose flour, almond flour, and baking powder together and then stir into the batter.
3. Grease and flour a round cake pan and pour the batter into it.
4. Cut each fig into 6 half-moon shaped pieces. Toss them with sugar and lemon juice. Press the figs gently into the batter in a circular pattern. Bake for about 30 minutes, or until the top of the cake is golden and a toothpick inserted in the middle comes out dry.
5. Let the cake cool. Melt the butter for the glaze in a small saucepan over low heat. Remove it from the heat and add in the rum and half of the powdered sugar. Whisk to a smooth consistency, adding some more confectioner's sugar if the glaze looks a bit thin. Pour the warm glaze over the cake slowly to let the cake absorb it all.

Boom! Crispy Pie!

The key to a great pie is dough that stays crispy. There's nothing more disappointing than when a pie looks crispy and delicious, but is deceivingly soggy when you bite into it. So I've learned this trick from the *school of pie hard knocks*, so to speak, since I myself have experienced a few pie-tastrophes over the years. My trick is to boil the sugar and flavorings, such as cardamom, cinnamon, or vanilla, before I mix it with the fruit. Boom! Crispy pie on the top and the bottom!

Crust:

4½ oz. butter, chilled

1 cup all-purpose flour

½ tsp. salt

2 – 3 tbsp. ice cold water

Filling:

¾ cup sugar

¼ vanilla bean, or 1 tbsp. vanilla extract

½ tsp. cardamom, ground

½ cup water

Juice of ½ lemon

3 tbsp. brandy

10 fresh apricots

Glazing:

1 egg

2 tbsp. raw sugar

To serve:

Whipped cream

Makes 1 tart; serves 6 to 8.

Brandied *Apricot Galette*

1. Start with the crust. You can always buy a crust if you're strapped for time, but a homemade crust will always beat a store-bought one in flavor.
2. Put the butter into a food processor and add in the flour and salt. Quickly mix for a minute to make the crumbly, dry dough. If it's not perfectly blended, that's ok.
3. Pour in the water and mix quickly at high speed until it becomes a ball. It's best to work the dough as little as possible.
4. Wrap the dough in plastic wrap and let it chill for at least 20 minutes in the fridge.
5. Make the filling. Split the vanilla bean in half length-wise. In a medium saucepan, bring the sugar, vanilla bean and seeds, cardamom, and water to a boil. Let it simmer to a thick syrup for about 10 minutes over medium heat. When the mix has thickened, add in lemon juice and brandy. Simmer for another minute, then remove from the heat and let cool.
6. Rinse, clean, and cut the apricots in half. Toss out the pits. Add the apricots to the cooling syrup.
7. Preheat the oven to 375°F.
8. Remove the crust from the refrigerator and set it down on a lightly floured surface. Roll the crust out to make a circle a fifth of an inch in thickness and 8 to 10 inches in diameter. It doesn't have to be perfect.
9. Place the crust on a sheet pan lined with parchment paper, pour the apricot filling into the middle of the crust, and fold the crust's edges up around the filling so only a small amount of the filling shows.
10. Beat the egg in a small cup to an egg wash. Brush the folded edges with the beaten egg wash and sprinkle with raw sugar. Bake the tart for about 20 to 25 minutes, or until the edges have turned golden brown and the apricots are soft. Serve with whipped cream.

Croissant & *Bourbon Bread Pudding*

2 croissants, preferably a few days old

¾ cup brown sugar

¼ cup milk

¼ cup whipping cream

2 tbsp. bourbon

2 eggs

Serves 4.

1. Preheat the oven to 325°F. Butter a small, ovenproof baking pan and pull the croissant apart into chunks and place in the pan.
2. Boil the sugar and 2 tablespoons of milk in a small saucepan for about 5 minutes, or until the sugar has melted and is turning to caramel. Remove the pan from the heat and add in the remaining milk, the cream, and the bourbon. Bring to a boil over low heat. Remove the pan from heat and let the caramel cool down until it's lukewarm.
3. Beat the eggs in bowl. Slowly pour the warm cream mixture into the bowl, a little at a time, whisking continuously. Then pour this mixture over the croissants and let sit for about 15 minutes so it will absorb the liquid. Bake the croissant pudding for 20 minutes. Let it cool for a few minutes before serving.

Apple *Upside-Down* Tart

2 tart apples

¾ cup brown sugar

4 tbsp. water

2 tbsp. ground cardamom

1 tbsp. butter

Juice of ½ lemon

1 sheet store-bought puff pastry

TIP!
The best apple pies are always made with tart apples.

1. Pour sugar and water into a small saucepan and simmer over low heat. Add cardamom and butter. Simmer for about 10 minutes, or until the mixture is a thick syrup.
2. Preheat the oven to 375°F.
3. Wash the apples and remove the stems. Cut the apples into super thin slices—by all means use a mandolin if you have one. Remove the seeds, but leave the core intact. Place the slices in a large bowl and squeeze the lemon juice over them. Shake the bowl to ensure that the slices are covered with the lemon juice.
4. Set the sheet of puff pastry on a lightly floured counter top and roll it out so that it fits gently into your round baking pan.
5. Butter the baking pan and layer the apple slices in a decorative pattern. Pour the cardamom syrup over the apples and cover them with the pastry dough.
6. Bake the tart on the middle rack of the oven for about 25 minutes. The tart is ready when the syrup bubbles around the edges and the pastry is golden brown.
7. Remove the tart from the oven and turn it over immediately (so it's apple-side up) onto a serving platter.

1 tart; serves 8 to 10.

S'mores
Pie

1 piecrust (see page 123)

7 oz. dark chocolate

¾ cup brown sugar

½ tsp. salt

1 tsp. vanilla extract

2 egg yolks

5 tbsp. all-purpose flour

1 cup milk

1 tbsp. butter

10 marshmallows

1 tart; serves 8.

1. Preheat the oven to 350°F.
2. Roll out the pastry dough and transfer it to a pie tin. Line the bottom as well as the sides of the pan with the dough. Prick the bottom of the pan with a fork and bake the crust for about 20 minutes, until the pastry is golden and flakey.
3. Use the broil function of your oven.
4. Chop the chocolate into pieces. Place the salt, vanilla extract, milk, and flour in a saucepan. Bring to a boil over low heat while stirring. Remove from heat. Beat the egg yolks in a bowl and slowly pour the warm milk into the eggs while still stirring.
5. Return the mixture to the saucepan and bring to a simmer over low heat for about 15 seconds. Remove the pan from the heat and add in the chopped chocolate and the butter. Using a spatula, stir until everything is well blended. This mixture will not thicken further while it bakes so make sure it is properly thickened beforehand.
6. Pour the chocolate mix into the piecrust and let it cool completely.
7. Cover the surface with marshmallows. Broil for about 5 to 10 minutes or until the marshmallows have melted and are crunchy.

More Gere

The leafy forests of *upstate* New York made for a disorienting drive on my way to the Bedford Post Inn, a bed and breakfast owned by none other than Mister Richard Gere. I was heading up there to cook with the star in his new hotel and restaurant, a refurbished old house that was once a stop along the route of *The Pony Express*. Though I thought I was lost at some points, I knew I was on the right track when I saw a group of camera-wielding, autograph-hunting Japanese women in front of me.

Gere had really good moves in the kitchen and was very particular about his olive oil and his ovens. The detail he was most passionate about, however, was lighting. At every table in his restaurant, he put up a little pink light— a trick from the movie business that makes everybody look at least ten years younger and at least 10% better. Needless to say, I have since stolen this trick for my own events.

Pound Cake
Trifle

1 pound cake
(see recipe on next page)

½ cup good quality
raspberry jam

1 cup raspberry liqueur,
such as Framboise

1⅓ cups raspberries

1⅓ cups strawberries

Lemon custard
(see recipe on next page)

1 cup heavy cream

1 tbsp. sugar

1 tsp. vanilla extract

1. Cut the cake into ¾-inch thick slices and spread the raspberry jam onto each slice. Set aside.
2. Set a layer of pound cake slices into a glass serving bowl with the sides smeared with jam facing up. Cut the slices to size to make them fit snuggly. Drizzle some Framboise over the slices. Add a layer of raspberries, then strawberries, and lastly lemon custard.
3. Repeat with another layer, and keep layering until the bowl is filled. Finish with a top layer of pound cake slices, jam-side down. Spread a layer of lemon custard on top. Let the cake sit for a while.
4. Whip the cream with sugar and vanilla extract and cover the top of the trifle with whipped cream.

Pound Cake

7 oz. butter, room temperature

1¾ cups brown sugar

4 large eggs

2½ cups all-purpose flour

½ tsp. baking powder

1 tsp. salt

1 tsp. vanilla extract

½ cup milk

½ cup crème fraîche

1. Preheat the oven to 350°F. Butter and flour two small loaf pans, about 6 inches long.
2. With a handheld electric mixer, beat butter, vanilla extract, and sugar airy and light. It'll take about 5 minutes. Add in the eggs, one at a time.
3. Sift flour, baking powder, and salt into a large bowl to remove any clumps. Mix milk and the crème fraîche in a smaller bowl. Stir some of the flour mix into the egg and butter batter, then some of the crème fraîche mixture into the egg and butter batter. Keep alternating until all is incorporated.
4. Pour the batter into the loaf pans. Bake for 45 to 60 minutes, or until a toothpick inserted into the middle of the cake comes out dry.
5. Let the cakes cool for about 10 minutes. Turn them out of the pans and let them cool on a baking rack. Cover with plastic wrap and store them in the refrigerator.

Lemon Custard

1¾ cup whipping cream

1 cup sugar

½ tbsp. vanilla extract

Peel from 1 lemon, finely grated

8 egg yolks

1. Heat cream, sugar, vanilla, and lemon peel in a saucepan. Bring to a boil, remove from the heat, and let the mixture stand until it reaches room temperature.
2. When the mixture has cooled down, add in the yolks while stirring. Warm over low heat while stirring continuously until the mixture has thickened and become thick like custard. Immediately remove the custard from the heat and keep stirring while it cools (or you'll end up with scrambled eggs).

1 cake; serves 12 to 15.

Late Night
Bites

a.k.a. *Drunchies*

Are you starving after a night out? Hitting a fast food joint in the middle of the night to grab something to go with your drink is as predictable as wings at the Super Bowl, beer on the Fourth of July, or Santa Claus at Christmas. But for everyone's sake, think again. Get rid of the questionable burgers and fries—remember the pink slime epidemic? Get your ass home and make a quick and delicious nighttime snack instead. Your wallet and your arteries will thank you. While you're at it, why not invite your friends home for an after-party? After all, the best part of any party is the after-party.

When you finally get home, throw open your refrigerator, release your inner chef, and run wild.

If you've got eggs, make some eggs in the hole. If you have rice, throw together a bowl of curried fried rice. None of the following recipes take more than 15 minutes to prepare. You'll probably spend more time correcting the cashier on your order at your favorite fast food joint than you will putting any of these recipes together. It'll taste better too, I promise. And hey, when you wake up the next morning you'll even have some leftovers for hangover munchies and can avoid that embarrassing walk of shame to the bodega on the corner.

As we all know, food tastes better late at night, especially after a drink or two.

No matter what type of gathering you're inviting people over for, don't forget to have a little something to snack on when the clock ticks closer to sunrise.

If you see a guy drunkenly poking around your kitchen, then you'll know you fucked up. So if you're throwing a party you suspect will go into the a.m., make sure to put out some food for your guests to munch on around midnight. You won't hear any complaints.

Red Spaghetti

2 servings spaghetti,
about 10 oz.

1 red onion

½ head radicchio salad

1 red beet

2 tbsp. butter

⅓ cup of walnuts

⅓ cup olive oil

Parmesan cheese, grated

Salt & freshly ground pepper

This recipe is a variation on the always-delicious pesto pasta, but has a slightly bitter taste. (For those of you who enjoy a gin and tonic now and then, this dish is for you!). However, watch out for spills because beets will stain everything they touch.

1. Cook the spaghetti according to instructions on the package.
2. Slice the red onion and chop the radicchio. Grate the beet.
3. Melt the butter in a saucepan. Add the beet, red onion, walnuts, and radicchio. Gently sauté for 5 minutes.
4. Using an immersion blender, mix the contents of the pan to a red pesto-like finish. Add in the olive oil and Parmesan cheese. Season with salt and pepper to taste.
5. Mix with the spaghetti and serve with additional Parmesan.

Serves 2.

Chive
Tagliatelle

3½ oz. melted butter

_____

2 bunches of chives

_____

1 egg yolk

_____

2 cups water

_____

10 oz. tagliatelle

_____

Salt & freshly ground pepper

1. Melt the butter in a saucepan and let it cool.
2. Finely chop the chives.
3. When the butter has cooled, whisk in the yolk. Heat over low heat while whisking continuously, until the mixture has thickened.
4. Cook the pasta according to the instructions on the package.
5. Drain off the pasta water. Mix the pasta with the butter and egg sauce and chives. Salt and pepper to taste.

Serves 2.

Curry
Fried Rice

This is the perfect recipe for using up those leftovers and it's a recipe my Dad gets all the *cred* for. His fried rice is famous in his 'hood, and he spices it up every time with some new ingredients – bad pun intended. So don't be shy— see what you've got in the refrigerator. Just about everything will fit the bill!

Serves 2.

Basic recipe:

3 tbsp. butter

1 tsp. curry powder

2 garlic cloves

1 yellow onion

1 tbsp. mushroom soy sauce

1¾ cup rice, cooked

1 tsp. sriracha sauce or ¼ tsp. cayenne pepper

2 large eggs

Salt & freshly ground pepper

1. Melt 1 tablespoon of butter in a skillet and add in half the curry. Chop the garlic and onion and add to the skillet. Now you simply add a bit of what you have in your refrigerator—chopped leftover chicken and bell pepper, for example—and sauté over medium heat. Remove from the heat and transfer it to a plate.
2. Place 2 tablespoons butter and the remaining curry in the skillet and heat it over high heat. Add the rice and fry it for about 5 minutes until crispy. Add in the sriracha sauce and break in the eggs. Season with salt and pepper. Stir and sauté for a minute or two longer. Add in the onion mixture and drizzle with the soy sauce. Serve it up.

TIP!
This recipe is a total kitchen cleaner-upper. You can add fried or grilled chicken, ham, bacon, bell peppers, or spinach.

Pan-Fried Bread
with Olive Oil– Marinated Tuna

This recipe was inspired by the food Mecca that is Italy. To be honest, I never really liked canned tuna until one evening in Sperlonga, in southern Italy. From my own inability to speak Italian and my waiter's comparable ineptitude in English, sprang a lively conversation that led to a platter of tuna fish I hadn't even realized I had ordered. Despite my own distaste for tuna fish and the horrific visions of smelly and stale sandwiches, the dish put my nightmares to shame. It was uuuhmazing!

4 thick slices bread, preferably stale
———————————————
2 tbsp. butter
———————————————
Olive oil
———————————————
½ oup cherry tomatoes
———————————————
½ red onion
———————————————
1 can tuna in olive oil
———————————————
¼ cup green olives, with pits
———————————————
Basil
———————————————
Salt & freshly ground pepper

1. Heat butter and olive oil in a skillet and pan fry the slices of bread over medium heat until they're golden brown and crunchy like croutons. Put to the side.
2. Cut the cherry tomatoes in half and slice the onion. Drain the tuna fish and mix it with tomatoes, red onion, olives, and some basil. Season with salt and pepper and add in olive oil. Toss gently and serve on the warm pan-fried bread.

Serves 2.

TIP!
For this salad you can add what you have on hand, for example, mozzarella cheese or artichoke hearts.

Truffle *Grilled Cheese*

One of the best creations ever to emerge from the American kitchen is the grilled cheese sandwich. When I lived in the States as a kid, my friends sneered at my brie-and-salami sandwiches in my lunchbox and no one wanted to trade with me. While the other kids were happily digging into PB & J's, my saving grace was the occasional classic grilled cheese sandwich that I brought.

TIP!

This stuff is great late night food to serve up to your guests if you are throwing a party. The dish can be made in advance and kept in the refrigerator. When ready to serve, simply reheat the sandwiches in the oven set at 350°F until the cheese has melted then serve immediately!

2 slices bread

2 tbsp. butter

1 tbsp. truffle oil

8 thick slices cheese; mix and match what you have at home, like cheddar

1. Butter one side of each slice of bread. Drizzle truffle oil over the other side.
2. Place the cheese on the side with the truffle oil, buttered side facing out. Place the two slices of bread together with the cheese in the middle to make a sandwich.
3. Heat a skillet over low heat. Add the sandwich and pan fry it slowly to allow the cheese to melt, about 4 to 5 minutes on each side until the surface is golden. Tip! If you're hungry for more, this sandwich goes really amazing with a tomato soup combo.

Makes 1 sandwich.

This is my favorite nighttime snack. It also serves as an excellent brunch dish the morning after the night out.

Serves 2; makes 4 sandwiches.

4 thick slices of bread

4 tbsp. butter

4 large eggs

Salt & freshly ground pepper

1. Cut a hole in each slice of bread using the open side of a regular drinking glass.
2. Spread butter on both sides of the bread. Heat a skillet over medium heat, place the bread in the pan, and fry it until it starts getting golden. Break an egg over each hole in the slice of bread. Season with salt and pepper. Turn the heat down to low.
3. Cook the slices of bread until one side is golden and then turn and fry the other side (it takes about 3 minutes per side). Serve immediately.

Egg in the Hole

Curried Chicken *Toast*

1 cup boneless chicken, cubed

2 pieces baguette, or rolls

3 tbsp. olive oil

1 cup fresh spinach leaves

¼ cup mayonnaise

1 tsp. sriracha sauce

1 tbsp. curry powder

½ red onion, chopped

3 tbsp. crasins

Makes 2 to 3 sandwiches.

1. Toast the bread in the oven.
2. Heat 2 tablespoons of olive oil in a skillet over medium heat and sauté the chicken. You can also use leftover cooked or grilled chicken, in which case you only need to reheat it in the skillet.
3. Remove the skillet from the heat, add in the spinach, and stir it until it wilts. Add in the red onion. Add mayonnaise, sriracha sauce, and curry powder mixed with olive oil and combine well. Add in the cranberries. Spoon the chicken mix onto the bread.

Quick 'n Dirty Wings

Makes 3 servings (4 wings each)

12 chicken wings, fresh or frozen

½ cup all-purpose flour

1 pinch cayenne pepper

¾ cup oil, for frying

Salt & freshly ground pepper

1. Mix flour and spices in a large bowl. If the wings are frozen, defrost them slightly in the microwave. Place the wings in the bowl and shake them until the flour covers the wings completely.
2. Heat the oil in a deep skillet or a heavy pot over medium heat. Add the wings to the oil and fry them, 5 or so at a time, until golden brown - about 5 minutes per side.
3. Place the pan-fried wings in a bowl. Mix one of the sauces and pour it over the wings. Shake the bowl until the wings are well-coated with the sauce.

Even though wings are as much of an American staple as the Superbowl itself, it took me a while to finally muster up the courage to even taste *Buffalo Chicken Wings*. I wish I hadn't been so hesitant to try them though, because wings are simply the best. I haven't turned my back on them since!

Asian wings:

3 tbsp. hoisin sauce

2 tbsp. honey

2 tsp. mushroom soy sauce

2 tbsp. black pepper

1 tsp. sriracha sauce

2 tbsp. sesame seeds

1. Whisk all the ingredients together in a bowl. Pour the sauce over the deep-fried wings and shake to coat. Serve immediately.

Buffalo wings:

2 oz. butter

Hot sauce

1. Melt the butter, add in an equal amount of hot sauce, and you have buffalo sauce.
2. Pour the sauce over the deep fried wings and shake until they are well coated. Serve immediately.

Nutella
Mug Cake

4 tbsp. all-purpose flour

1 tsp. baking powder

4 tbsp. sugar

1 large egg

1 tsp. vanilla extract

3 tbsp. cacao powder

4 tbsp. Nutella

3 tbsp. milk

3 tbsp. melted butter

Sometimes late at night you don't want something greasy and salty at all, but rather something sweet and gooey—along the lines of dessert—in which case it's time to whip up this super easy recipe.

1. Mix all the ingredients together and pour them into two mugs, filling them three-quarters full. Place the mugs in the microwave and cook on the highest setting. The time required will depend on your microwave's power so start with 1 minute and then check. If you need to cook them more, add 20 seconds at a time. The cake should look baked on top. Serve right away

Serves 2.

Tips!

Prepare your midnight snacks ahead of time!

If you're hosting a party and want to serve something later on in the evening, remember to opt for dishes you can put together ahead of time that don't require much prep when it's time to eat. It's a pain in the ass to prepare something complicated when the festivities are at their height. One of my favorite late night party foods is actually pork belly (in the Family Style chapter). That recipe has been a hit countless times.

Relax about your diet already!

It's time to party and not the time to freak out about your diet. As I'm sure you know, a night spent knocking back cocktails will make your guests crave something greasy and artery-clogging, so forget the salads and low-calorie options and cook up something that will stick to their ribs!

Hot toddy!*

When it's cold outside, there's nothing cozier than a *hot toddy*. In wintertime, I often send my guests home for the night with a to-go cup of rich, hot cocoa with a shot of liquor, of course! You'll find the recipe for the toddy on page 41.

How many munchies?

Count 7 oz. of food per person—a bit more if most of the guests are guys.

What time?

Bring out the late-night snacks about 2 to 3 hours after the party food has been demolished by your guests. If dinner ended at 10 p.m., a good time to bring out round two would be around midnight.

Fake 'n Bake

Shortcuts, Smart Tips & Easy Recipes

People get worried whenever they invite a chef over for dinner that they are suddenly going to become a food critic as well. But let me tell you, in my experience, no one appreciates a home-cooked meal (that they didn't have to make themselves) more than a chef. Friends think I'll become a reality cooking competition show judge who'll critique their meal on levels of difficulty, presentation, creativity, and use of the weekly secret ingredients. I'm not Gordon Ramsay! We're all bound to fuck up in the kitchen, even the pros. The difference is, we've learned a few tricks along the way.

Let's face it: we can't all be Martha Stewart, with a butler and a bevy of assistants on call to help us lay out an ornate spread. Perhaps you're having your girlfriends over after work and you've just gotten your foot in the door or maybe it's your turn to make Sunday dinner and you haven't been to the grocery store in days. You shouldn't be tearing your hair out over what to eat. My solution: cheat.

After years of planning parties, dinners, and events, I've picked up a trick or twelve to help me out when shit hits the fan. In my business, more often than not, I'll be under pressure when faced with having to organize the perfect *dinner party*. It's totally okay to use a few shortcuts in food prep. So don't cancel your evening plans just yet. Make something *almost* homemade. One of my best moves is to fake a pizza: pick up a plain pizza from your local pizzeria. Bring it home and dress it up with prosciutto, a drizzle of truffle oil, and a couple of other ingredients. Pop it in the oven for a few minutes (see the recipe on page 152) and the pizza will taste like you just tossed the dough from scratch. Bask in the glory of your guests' praise - but dammit, don't forget to throw out the pizza box!

Truffle *Honey*

The cheese platter is a true workhorse of the trade and it has saved my ass many times. With just a few tricks you can make this platter both new and fresh.

½ cup honey

2 tbsp. truffle purée or oil

Sea salt & freshly ground pepper

1. Heat the honey gently on the stove or in the microwave and stir in the truffle purée. Season with salt and pepper.

TIP!
You can use just about any truffle product to give your honey some truffle flavor—truffle oil, truffle salt, or preserved truffle, for example. Make use of what you already have in your kitchen for this recipe. Whatever you choose will bring your cheese platter to new heights.

Charcuterie *Chips*

15 thin-cut slices salami or Spanish chorizo

15 thin slices dry-cured ham, such as prosciutto

1. Preheat the oven to 300°F. Spread out the salami and ham on separate baking sheets covered in parchment paper. Do not mix the two meats, as they will take on the other's flavors.
2. Bake the ham and chorizo in the oven for about 10 to 16 minutes, or until they are crisp to the touch.

30 pieces, enough for 4 to 6 servings.

I'm warning you: these chips will disappear in the blink of an eye!

Super
Hummus

Regular hummus is like Clark Kent, but this is Super Hummus. And it's the perfect finger food to serve with pita chips and veggie sticks.

Serves 4 to 6.

14 oz. store-bought hummus
_____

¼ tsp. cayenne pepper
_____

½ tsp. herb salt
_____

1 tsp. smoked paprika
_____

Juice from ¼ lemon
_____

2 tbsp. olive oil

1. Place the hummus in a bowl. Sprinkle with cayenne pepper, herb salt, and paprika. Squeeze the lemon juice onto it and drizzle with olive oil. Let the hummus sit for a few minutes, then serve it with some store-bought or homemade pita chips, see recipe below.

Homemade Pita Chips:

Serves 4 to 6.

It's even quicker to make homemade pita chips than it is to make hummus. Buy some hummus at the store and then tell all your guests about your great home-made pita chips.

8 pita breads
_____

½ cup olive oil
_____

2 tbsp. garlic powder
_____

2 tbsp. smoked paprika
_____

Salt & freshly ground pepper

1. Preheat the oven to 400°F. Cut the pita breads in half and place them in a large plastic freezer bag.
2. Mix the olive oil and the spices. Pour this mix over the pieces of pita in the bag a little at a time and shake the bag until all the oil has been absorbed by the pita. Spread the pieces of pita on a baking sheet and bake them in the oven for about 10 to 15 minutes, or until they're crispy. Serve the chips with hummus.

Crudité *Cups*

Simple crudité sauce:

1 clove garlic

Herb salt

1 tsp. lemon juice

1 tbsp. parsley, chopped

1 cup crème fraîche

½ tsp. tarragon, fresh or dried

To serve:
Vegetables

Crudité is probably the most simple finger food to offer your guests while you're busy in the kitchen. If you want a slightly classier look that coerces people into mingling, put some sauce into the bottom of the glass and place the crudités on top.

1. Peel and coarsely chop the garlic. Place it in a mortar and add just a little bit of salt. Mash the garlic and salt with the pestle until it becomes a paste. Add lemon, tarragon, and parsley, and mash again. Mix in the crème fraîche and season with salt.
2. Serve the sauce with raw vegetables, such as cauliflower or broccoli florets; carrot and celery sticks; asparagus spears and green, or wax, beans.

Serves 4 to 6.

Faux-made *pizzas*

Most New Yorkers will tell you that the secret to the city's fantastic pizza (and bagels for that matter) is the tap water. My favorite last-minute pie is by the Italian couple that owns *Pizza No 28* on Carmine Street. Their thin-crust pizzas are more European style than regular New York pizzas, which have a somewhat thicker crust. If I'm not in the mood to put together a pizza of my own or I don't have the time (a more likely issue), I call them up and order a pizza and throw my own toppings on it before serving.

Truffle *Pizza*

Makes 1 pizza; serves 2.

1 plain cheese pizza

1 tbsp. olive oil

1 cup mixed mushrooms
(such as button mushrooms
and shiitake)

½ cup grated mozzarella

½ cup Parmesan, grated

2 tbsp. truffle oil

Freshly ground pepper

1. Preheat the oven to 450°F. Heat a skillet with 1 tablespoon of oil over medium heat. Clean, slice, and sauté the mushrooms.
2. Spread the mushrooms and cheese over the pizza. Finish by drizzling the truffle oil over the pizza and then season with pepper.
3. Bake until the cheese has melted and is bubbling, about 5 to 10 minutes. Serve hot and crispy.

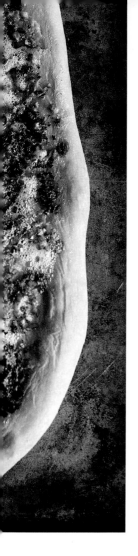

Pear and Gorgonzola *Pizza*

Makes 1 pizza; serves 2.

1 plain cheese pizza

7 oz. Gorgonzola

1 handful hazelnuts

10 slices dry-cured ham, such a prosciutto

1 pear

1. Preheat the oven to 450°F. Crumble the Gorgonzola, chop the hazelnuts, and sprinkle them over the pizza. Bake for 5 to 10 minutes, or until the Gorgonzola is melted.
2. Cut the pear into thin slices and layer it, along with the ham, on the pizza. Serve immediately.

Fish
Tacos

1 ¼ lb. fish fillet, such as cod, hake, or mahi mahi

½ cup all-purpose flour

Salt

1 pinch cayenne pepper

½ cup oil, for frying

8 tortillas

1 avocado

Cabbage salad:

1 cup red cabbage, sliced thin

3 spring onions or scallions, sliced thin

Juice from ½ lime

1 tsp. sriracha sauce

2 tbsp. olive oil

Salt & freshly ground pepper

Spicy mayo:

¼ cup mayonnaise

2 tbsp. sriracha sauce

Salt

Believe it or not, New York somehow has a ton of dedicated surfers who head out to the coast of Long Island every weekend. One of the most popular taco shacks is *Rockaway Taco at Rockaway Beach.*

1. Start by making the onion and cabbage slaw. Whisk together lime juice, sriracha sauce, olive oil, salt, and pepper in a large bowl. Stir in the cabbage and spring onions. Set aside.
2. Make the spicy mayonnaise by mixing mayonnaise and sriracha sauce. Season to taste with salt.
3. Cut the fish into 4-inch pieces. Mix flour and spices, then roll the fish in the flour mixture. Heat the oil in a deep, heavy pan and pan-fry the fish.
4. Warm up the tortillas. Remove the pit, peel, and slice the avocado. Serve the tortilla with onion and cabbage slaw, pan-fried fish, and avocado drizzled with spicy mayo.

Serves 4.

I found out the secret to making authentic guacamole straight from the source, a.k.a. a local little old lady cooking in a cactus field in Jalisco, Mexico. I was there to attend tequila school hosted by a local blue agave farmer. Surrounded by ten hungry vaqueros (Mexican cowboys) and me, the 80-year-old woman explained to me the common mistake all *gringos* make when making guacamole is forgetting to put in garlic and chili peppers and crush it all with a mortar and pestle. Yes, the secret to great guac is garlic and a mortar.

2 avocados

¼ yellow onion

½ clove garlic

¼ jalapeño pepper

Salt

1 lime, juice of

1. Chop the onion, garlic, and jalapeño pepper. Place the garlic and jalapeño in a mortar and add a pinch of salt. Crush the garlic and pepper to the consistency of purée with the pestle.
2. Add the onion and some more salt. Continue crushing with the pestle.
3. Peel the avocado and remove the stone. Place it in the mortar and mash it with a fork. Squeeze half the lime over the avocado, taste, and add more lime to taste.
4. Serve with tortilla chips.

Homemade tortilla chips:

10 tortillas

1 cup oil, for frying

Salt

1. Cut the tortillas into wedges.
2. Heat the oil over medium heat in a deep, heavy pan. Test the heat by slipping a wedge of tortilla into the oil. The oil is hot enough if the oil begins to bubble and the tortilla turns golden.
3. Deep-fry the tortilla wedges in batches until they float to the top of the oil's surface.
4. Place the chips in a paper bag, letting the bag absorb any excess oil. Add salt to the chips and shake the bag to spread the salt evenly over the chips. Serve.

Guac
for Gringos

The chips will keep for about 3 days and will taste good as new if you put them in the microwave for 30 seconds before serving.

Serves 2.

Kale Caesar
with
Homemade Dressing

Serves 3 to 4.

1. Remove any coarse stems from the kale and coarsely chop the leaves. Debone the chicken and chop the meat. Place everything in a large bowl.
2. Finely chop the anchovies and transfer them to a smaller bowl. Add in pressed garlic, Dijon mustard, lemon juice, and egg yolks. Whisk thoroughly.
3. While whisking, slowly pour the oil into the anchovy-egg mixture. Season with salt and pepper and add in the Parmesan cheese.
4. Pour half of the dressing over the kale and the chicken and toss to cover. Let the salad sit in the refrigerator until mealtime to let the flavors develop. Add a bit more dressing to the salad before serving it, but save some for drizzling at the table. Serve with croutons.

2 bunches kale

1 whole grilled chicken

2 anchovy fillets

1 garlic clove

1 tbsp. Dijon mustard

2 tbsp. lemon juice

2 egg yolks

1 cup olive oil

½ cup Parmesan, grated finely

Salt & freshly ground pepper

To serve:

½ cup croutons

Chicken salad:

1 grilled chicken

1 red onion

¼ cup almonds
(preferably marcona)

½ cup crème fraîche

½ cup aïoli

2 tbsp. curry powder

1 tbsp. sriracha sauce (or a
pinch of cayenne pepper)

Salt & freshly ground pepper

Salad:

10½ oz. lettuce, such as mâche
or fresh spinach

1 avocado

1 handful green olives

Dressing:

2 tbsp. Dijon mustard

Juice of ½ lemon

¼ cup olive oil

Salt & freshly ground pepper

Salad
Salad

One day while I was
in the kitchen fixing
this dish, my boyfriend
walked by and asked,
surprised: "Are we ea-
ting salad with a salad?"
Hence, a new recipe
name was born! Salad
salad is definitely the
way to go when you're
in a hurry, but it's also
filling enough to work as
a light dinner.

Serves 3 to 4.

1. Debone tho chicken and cut the meat into cubes. Transfer it
   a large bowl.
2. Chop the red onion and almonds and mix them with the
   chicken. Mix in the crème fraîche, aïoli, curry powder, sriracha
   sauce, salt, and pepper. Set aside while you prepare the
   second salad.
3. Rinse and dry the lettuce and place it on a large platter. Peel
   the avocado and remove the stone. Slice the avocado over
   the lettuce and add the olives.
4. Combine all the ingredients for the dressing and whisk them
   with a fork until the dressing has thickened. Drizzle the dressing
   over the green salad and serve it with the chicken salad.

4 apples

¾ cup sugar

1 tbsp. ground cinnamon

1 tsp. ground cardamom

2 sheets puff pastry, defrosted

All-purpose flour

1 large egg

To serve:

Vanilla ice cream

Apple *Puffs*

1. Preheat the oven to 400°F. Mix sugar, cinnamon, and cardamom in a bowl. Set aside.
2. Peel and core the apples, leaving the apples whole. Remove the core to make a hole straight through the middle.
3. Roll out the puff pastry on a lightly floured work surface. Cut the sheets into 4 square pieces.
4. Brush the edges of each square of pastry with egg wash, set the apple down in the middle of the square, and fill the center hole with the sugar and spice mix. Take a hold of the pastry's edges and pinch them closed around the apple. Repeat with the other three apples.
5. Put the apples in the freezer for 15 minutes, then place them on a sheet pan and brush them with the remaining egg wash. Bake the apples for 5 minutes. Lower the oven's temperature to 350°F and bake for another 20 minutes, or until the pastry is golden. Be careful not to over-bake the apples or the puffs might fall apart. Serve them warm with vanilla ice cream.

Serves 4.

Raspberry
Fool

1 cup raspberries,
fresh or frozen

1 tsp. finely grated lemon peel

½ cup sugar

1 cup heavy cream

½ cup crème fraîche

Serves 4 to 6

1. If using frozen raspberries, defrost them. Mix raspberries, lemon peel, and a generous one fourth cup of the sugar. Mash it all with a fork. Set aside.
2. Whip the cream and the remaining sugar with an electric mixer until it increases in volume and stiff peaks form. Stir in the crème fraîche.
3. Layer the cream and raspberries in decorative glasses. Serve.

TIP!
Try this with toasted sponge cake. Cut slices of cake and toast them lightly in a toaster.

Make The Oven Your New Best Friend.

It's much easier to make a dish ahead of time when you can just put it in the oven instead of cooking it in a pan. Choose a recipe where you can put food in the oven and leave it until you're ready to eat. Enjoy a glass of wine with a friend in the meantime and simply wait for the timer to go off.

Store-bought sauces?

I have nothing against store-bought sauces, but you can spice them up. Try adding some fresh herbs and you'll instantly turn your pre-made sauce into something fresh and homemade.

So Many People to Thank and Only One Page

Karolina Urbanska, my sounding board and the ultimate foil to my dyslexia: Thank you for spending days with me checking through my writing and my ideas and for helping me express myself when I had a hard time finding the right words. You and Henrik are cooler than the other side of the pillow and I hope you'll never get tired of me.

Per Faustino: You, too, are cooler than the other side of the pillow. Thank you for letting me put together a book that's about as close to what I could ever dream up and for guiding this project from beginning to end with your capable team at Nordstedts. Many thanks also go to Gabriella and Johanna for all your hard work!

Dan MacMahon, photographer extraordinaire, took all the wonderful photos of the people and the parties. You saw details in there that others might have missed. The world is a far more beautiful place through your camera lens. I want to live in your world!

Tove Eklund, the fantastic illustrator of this book. You're not only a wonderful artist, you're also one of my oldest and dearest friends. I've watched you paint and draw since I was 4 years old and it always felt shitty when you displayed a piece of art while I proudly held up a stick figure. I'm so happy that your sense of humor and your talent are an integral part of this book.
Adrian Mueller & Tadeu Magalhaes: Thank you for your invaluable work on this book and the many long hours you devoted to putting this book together. A girl couldn't ask for a better team.

Everyone at the publishers' who has been involved in the production of the book, whether they originally set out to be or not: Nicole Frail, Kajsa Berglund, Frida Jeppsson, Ciera Jones—Thank you!

Thank you to my family: Dad Peter, Mom Margareta, and Step-Dad Mats! You've always been incredibly supportive and encouraging. Mom: You're not only smart and insatiably curious, but you're also wise. Thank you for letting me march to the beat of my own drum and for not balking, but believing in even my most hare-brained schemes. Thank you for sending me out into the world with a little more self-confidence than I deserved. When I grow up, Mom, I want to be just like you.

Many thanks to my New York family: I am lucky to have a boyfriend who doesn't care if I miss a few weekends "because I have to work" and he loves me even though he had to attend most of his office Christmas parties solo. Daniel Walsh, your support means the world to me, and without it, this book (and many other projects) would not have been possible. I can't tell you how much I appreciate it. *Dan, you're my man!* I have the best friends—we've spent over 12 years in New York celebrating many holidays together and being homesick together. You know me, through and through, and I feel we're a true family. Jennifer Ohlsson, Camilla Thorsson, Signe Nordström, Lindsay Cox, and Lisa Tobias: Love you guys!*

Thanks to all my gorgeous and hungry friends who ate and modeled like total pros. And who showed up even when the photo session took place on a rainy Monday: Jesse, Camilla, Henry, Jennifer, Ksenyea, Lisa, Eric, Jingle, Jared, Justin, Amy, Lorenzo, Mitch, Sofia, Niklas, Kajsa, Frida, Signe, Kelly, Anushka, Andres, Lily, Stacy, Mari, Claire, Adam, Tony, Cat lil' Doug, little L, and of course, Dan.

Mateus, you were always ready to lend me your fine tableware for the pictures taken both in Europe and in the US. Teresa, Maria, and Filippa, *you rock!*

Thanks to Face Stockholm and to Lauren for the wonderful make-up: you're the best!

Royal Copenhagen and ABC Carpet: Thank you for lending me your fantastic china.

I'd also like to thank all those who have worked and teamed up with me, who have employed me or inspired me over these past years in New York. I still remember how it felt to land in the big city as a naïve, twenty-year-old, blue-eyed babe-in-the-woods, when nobody wanted to speak to me, let alone hire me. I'm sincerely grateful for your support.

Copy Assistant: **Karolina Urbanska, Alex Lordahl**
Assistants: **Kajsa Berglund, Frida Jeppsson**
Make-up: **Lauren Conklin/Face Stockholm**

Menu Suggestions For Different Occasions:

Friday *Nights with Friends*

1. Fish Tacos
2. Guac for Gringos with homemade tortilla chips

Cocktail *Party*

1. Sriracha Popcorn
2. Charcuterie Chips
3. Lobster Rolls
4. Crudité Cups
5. Preserved Lemon Chicken Salad
6. Rum Raisin Ice Cream Sandwiches
7. Pie Pops

Buffet

1. Spicy Cheese Sticks
2. Bacon & Leek Quiche
3. Hoisin Barbecued Pork Belly
4. Warm Tomato Salad with Burrata
5. Lady Cake

Last−minute *Dinners*

1. Truffle Pizza
2. Hazelnut & Parmesan Kale
3. Raspberry Fool

Sunday *Dinner*

1. Oven-Roasted Chicken with Calvados & Lady Apples
2. Spicy Peach Chutney
3. Oven-Roasted Carrots with Curry Oil & Fennel Seeds
4. Hurricane Chocolate Cake

Conversion Charts
METRIC AND IMPERIAL CONVERSIONS

(These conversions are rounded for convenience)

Ingredient	Cups/Tablespoons/ Teaspoons	Ounces	Grams/Milliliters
Butter	1 cup=16 tablespoons= 2 sticks	8 ounces	230 grams
Cream cheese	1 tablespoon	0.5 ounce	14.5 grams
Cheese, shredded	1 cup	4 ounces	110 grams
Cornstarch	1 tablespoon	0.3 ounce	8 grams
Flour, all-purpose	1 cup/1 tablespoon	4.5 ounces/0.3 ounce	125 grams/8 grams
Flour, whole wheat	1 cup	4 ounces	120 grams
Fruit, dried	1 cup	4 ounces	120 grams
Fruits or veggies, chopped	1 cup	5 to 7 ounces	145 to 200 grams
Fruits or veggies, puréed	1 cup	8.5 ounces	245 grams
Honey, maple syrup, or corn syrup	1 tablespoon	.75 ounce	20 grams
Liquids: cream, milk, water, or juice	1 cup	8 fluid ounces	240 milliliters
Oats	1 cup	5.5 ounces	150 grams
Salt	1 teaspoon	0.2 ounces	6 grams
Spices: cinnamon, cloves, ginger, or nutmeg (ground)	1 teaspoon	0.2 ounce	5 milliliters
Sugar, brown, firmly packed	1 cup	7 ounces	200 grams
Sugar, white	1 cup/1 tablespoon	7 ounces/0.5 ounce	200 grams/12.5 grams
Vanilla extract	1 teaspoon	0.2 ounce	4 grams

OVEN TEMPERATURES

Fahrenheit	Celcius	Gas Mark
225°	110°	¼
250°	120°	½
275°	140°	1
300°	150°	2
325°	160°	3
350°	180°	4
375°	190°	5
400°	200°	6
425°	220°	7
450°	230°	8